Cecily Layzell

walk & eat

AMSTE

CONTENTS

This pocket guide is designed for short-break walking holidays based in Amsterdam, using public transport. The city is easily reached by several (budget) airlines and the Eurostar via Brussels. Many visitors come to Amsterdam for a long weekend but there is more than enough to do for a week. You have in your hands enough walks, excursions, restaurants and recipes to last almost two weeks — so you can pick and choose the most appealing.

The highlights at a glance:

- 11 walks, 10 in the city itself, another in the countryside
- 2 excursions — enjoyable in their own right for the 'sights', but even more so for the walking opportunities
- recommended cafés, restaurants and bars along each route
- 10 Dutch recipes you can easily make yourself
- hints on wheat-, gluten- and dairy-free eating and cooking in Amsterdam

INTRO

THE WALKS

With a compact, historic centre, pedestrian-friendly canals, parks and relatively little traffic, Amsterdam is a walker's paradise. As a capital city, it is a year-round destination and there is always something to do. Each of the 10 city walks covers a different neighbourhood and includes several points of interest; combined, they provide a good overview and take in all the major sights and museums (where you may want to stop en route), as well as plenty of spots off the beaten track. All the walks are easy and can be undertaken at any time of year.

One longer walk starts in Castricum, a town about 40km northwest of Amsterdam. It is on the edge of the North Holland Dune Reserve, one of the country's largest areas of natural beauty, and you can walk — again, all year round — through the flora- and fauna-rich reserve to the bustling coastal town of Egmond aan Zee. Cool off with a dip in the North Sea, stroll along the boulevard or dine at one of the many seafront restaurants.

The book is designed for visitors using public transport. Most of the walks are in or close to the city centre, or you can reach the starting point within a few minutes on the city's efficient, integrated network of buses, trams and metros (underground). Car hire is *not* recommended: parking is expensive and, particularly in the centre, can be almost impossible to find. Reversing into a tiny spot on the edge of a canal can also be daunting, even for local residents, as evidenced by the 30 or so vehicles that end up in the water each year!

THE EXCURSIONS

I have outlined two excursions outside the city. The first is to Muiden, a picturesque historic village a short bus ride east of Amsterdam and home to Muiderslot, a medieval castle at the mouth of the River Vecht. The castle itself makes for an interesting visit, but there is also a scenic 10km walk from Muiden to the village of Muiderberg and back again along an old sea dike. The second excursion visits the Kröller-Müller Museum, with a fantastic collection of impressionist and post-impressionist paintings and sculptures. As a bonus, it's located in the heart of the Hoge Veluwe National Park, with a wealth of walking opportunities.

THE RESTAURANTS AND CAFÉS

Amsterdam has long been a city known for its hedonistic rather than gastronomic pleasures. In recent years, however, a new generation of chefs has focused on updating traditional dishes, bringing back so-called 'forgotten' ingredients, and experimenting with unusual taste combinations. This has resulted in a lively culinary scene to rival southern neighbours Belgium and France — if you know where to look!

I have included details of some of the best or most representative restaurants and cafés to be found along the walks. All are open year-round, although it is worth noting that many places are closed on Sunday and/or Monday, and it is still relatively rare to find kitchens open later than 10pm. It is advisable to reserve a table in advance, especially at weekends.

Each featured restaurant has been given a price guide, from € (relatively inexpensive) to €€€ (quite pricey). *No restaurant has paid, in cash or in kind, to be included in this guide.* For additional dining ideas, visit www.eat-amsterdam.com, a busy English-language website packed with restaurant listings, reviews and food-related news.

THE RECIPES

The majority of the restaurants I approached for recipes were happy to share both the ingredients and preparation with me. However, I *did* cook all the recipes myself, just to make sure they work (most of the photographs are my own results).

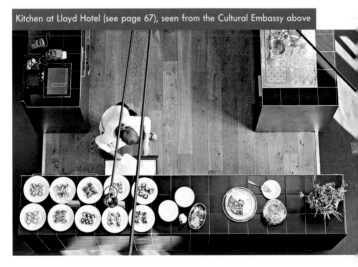

Kitchen at Lloyd Hotel (see page 67), seen from the Cultural Embassy above

What I cannot guarantee, of course, is that they will taste as good back home as they did in Amsterdam! So many factors come into play to make food taste better when you are on holiday, from your relaxed state of mind and appetite after a good walk, to the variety and quality of the products used. This is why I endorse self-catering (see page 11), so you can try out some of the recipes while you are still in Amsterdam.

Most of the recipes featured are simple to prepare and based on no-nonsense culinary traditions, simple cooking facilities and readily available ingredients. Where specifically Dutch ingredients are required, I have also provided the Dutch word and suggestions of where to find them. For information on **gluten- and dairy-free** cooking and eating, see page 138.

PLANNING YOUR VISIT
When to go

Amsterdam has plenty to offer at any time of year. Accommodation prices are highest and the city most crowded in July and August, although **high season** starts in April (when visitors flock to see the tulips in bloom and join the nationwide street party celebrating the Queen's official birthday on 30 April) and runs to September. December is also busy, particularly around the 31st when the Dutch welcome the **New Year** quite literally with a bang.

There is no guarantee of good weather, even in the summer, but when the sun does shine temperatures rarely exceed 25°C/ 77°F. In the **winter** it is more often grey and damp than cold, although the winds whipping off the North Sea can be biting.

This might make sightseeing less appealing, but will give you plenty of excuses to dive into cosy cafés to warm up. The best time to visit is **spring** or **autumn**, when temperatures are mild and queues manageable. Some museums shorten their opening hours between October and March, particularly the smaller ones, but few close completely.

Food-related events to look out for during the year include the biannual **Amsterdam Restaurant Week**, held in spring and late summer/autumn. Over the course of a week, hundreds of restaurants serve a special three-course lunch for €20 or three-course dinner for €25. Reservations open about three weeks prior to the event on www.restaurantweek.nl, and if you are quick you may be able to snap up a table at a top restaurant. In June, the city hosts **Taste of Amsterdam**. Alongside cooking demonstrations and workshops, this four-day culinary festival also offers plenty of opportunities to sample local food and drink (www.tasteofamsterdam.nl).

Festivals & public holidays

Accommodation might be tight and businesses closed during major festivals and holidays:
- 30 April: Queen's Day (a massive street party celebrating Queen Beatrix's official birthday)
- Apr/May/Jun: Ascension Day
- May/Jun: Pentecost (Whit Sunday and Monday)
- August: Gay Pride (usually the first weekend of the month)
- November: International Documentary Film Festival Amsterdam
- 5 December: Sinterklaas (Saint Nicholas — the day Dutch children traditionally receive presents)
- 25 December: Christmas Day
- 26 December: Boxing Day
- 1 January: New Year's Day

Getting there

Amsterdam is very well served by **flights** from the UK and many European countries. Royal Dutch Airlines (KLM, www.klm.com) is the national carrier, with flights from several airports including London (Heathrow and City), Cardiff, Bristol, Manchester, Newcastle, Glasgow and Edinburgh; British Airways (www.britishairways.com) operates from London (Heathrow, Gatwick and City airports), Manchester, Glasgow and Edinburgh. A number of low-cost airlines, including Ryanair, EasyJet, BMI Baby, Transavia and Jet2.com, fly from airports all over the UK, although some flights are to Eindhoven or Rotterdam rather than Amsterdam. Check the individual websites for exact details.

Travelling overland with **Eurostar** from London is an attractive option. Reasonably priced tickets can be found if you book in advance and, unlike air travel, the train will deliver you from city centre to city centre. The entire journey takes about six hours with a change in Brussels, but considering the time needed to get to the airport and longer check-in times due to increased security, this is not that much more than flying.

It is also possible to take the **ferry** from Harwich to Rotterdam (www.stenaline.co.uk), Hull to Rotterdam (www.poferries.com) and Newcastle to Ijmuiden/Amsterdam (www.dfdsseaways.co.uk).

Where to stay

As you would expect of a capital city, there is a wide choice of **hotels** of all grades in Amsterdam. A quick search on the internet will bring back hundreds of options. Rather than a hotel, however, consider staying in an **apartment**. There are a number of options, conveniently located in the city centre, which offer more space and freedom than a hotel and often end up being cheaper, particularly if you use their cooking facilities and eat in occasionally. Stay Amsterdam (www.stayamsterdam.com) has over 100 short-let properties. These range from two-person maisonettes to family houses with a private garden. All are furnished to a high standard and come with a fully equipped kitchen and bathroom. Some also have internet access and laundry facilities.

For something a bit different, try a **bed and breakfast**. These are generally not as economical as they are in other countries, but often offer a unique experience in terms of design or location. Le Maroxidien (www.lemaroxidien.com) is on a houseboat docked just a 10-minute walk from Central Station. The three colourful guest rooms have been

Room and kitchen at Le Maroxidien, a colourfully decorated houseboat 10 minutes from Central Station

carefully furnished in the style of Morocco, India and Mexico, and an organic breakfast is served each morning in the large dining room with views of the passing ducks.

What to take

Pack simply. You don't need to dress up for dinner in Amsterdam, although the very high-end restaurants would probably appreciate it if you were neatly attired.

If you are arriving by car or train, a small bag or suitcase should suffice. With charges increasingly levied for hold luggage, particularly by budget airlines, and often long waiting times at baggage reclaim, if you are flying I recommend taking hand luggage only if possible. But do check the hand luggage allowances and restrictions for your airline before you leave! New regulations on liquids, for example, could affect which toiletries you pack, and airlines can deny you boarding if your hand luggage exceeds a stipulated weight or size. In addition, there are food restrictions between certain countries, so the chunk of Dutch cheese you bought as a souvenir may be confiscated at customs.

No special equipment is needed for the city walks — just comfortable **walking shoes**. But for longer Walk 11 in dune country, and for any walking during the two excursions, proper (waterproof) **walking boots** are best, as the paths may be muddy. A **sunhat** and high-protection **sun cream** are equally important for *all* the walks: there is little shade on some, and sunburn or even sunstroke is a real risk, especially between May and September. A **fold-up umbrella** can be useful in wet weather, but as the rain is frequently accompanied by blustery winds which will turn the umbrella inside out in minutes, a **wind- and waterproof jacket** with a hood is a better option.

The slow-moving water in Amsterdam's canals makes them fertile breeding grounds for mosquitoes, so **insect repellent** is useful in the warm months. Each of you should carry a small **rucksack**, so you can share the load. For the walks in the city you should not need to carry much except the few items listed above. But for Walk 11 and any walking on the two excursions, which take you into some sparsely populated areas, it is also advisable to carry a **first aid kit**, a whistle, torch, spare socks and bootlaces and some warm clothing. A long-sleeved top and long trousers should ideally be worn, for protection against the sun, insects and **ticks,** which can carry disease.

It is a good idea to carry **water** (at least half a litre per person, a litre in hot weather) even on the shorter walks. It is essential on longer walks and walks outside the city where cafés and restaurants are scarcer. Bottles of mineral water are available everywhere and, when empty, can be refilled from any tap.

Planning your walks

All the walks and excursions are designed to be easily accessible by Amsterdam's excellent **integrated public transport network** of trams, buses, metros, boats and trains.

The walks have been **graded** for the deskbound person who nevertheless keeps reasonably fit. My timings average 4km/2.5mi per hour. In such a flat country, none of the walks involves ascents or descents much longer or steeper than a canal bridge or dike, apart from the gently rolling dunes in Walk 11. Remember that these are only *walking times*; increase the overall time by at least 50 percent, to allow for any breaks, visits to museums and nature-watching.

Safety depends a great deal on knowing what to expect and being properly equipped. For this reason it is advisable to read the whole walk description before setting out. Most of the walks are easily manageable and in areas where you will encounter plenty of other people, so it is perfectly safe to walk alone. Walk 11 and walks from the excursion bases, however, are isolated in places. This does not mean you cannot tackle them alone, but do be alert and always let someone know where you are going. You may also consider carrying a mobile phone with you. The Dutch **emergency number is 112.**

All the walks are easy to follow, with frequent signs and distinctive landmarks. On the few occasions when this is not the case I have given additional directions.

Verifying timetables in advance

While transport details are given in the 'logistics' panel at the start of each walk, remember that these timetables were correct at the time of writing. The best way to verify departures and returns is using the excellent journey planners available on the web. All the websites mentioned below have English versions.

The majority of **trams, buses, metros** and **ferries** within Amsterdam are operated by GVB. Its website (www.gvb.nl) has details of maps, timetables, tickets and prices. There is also a GVB information office on Stationsplein in front of Central Station (open Mon-Fri 07.00-21.00; Sat-Sun 10.00-18.00). A couple of buses mentioned in this book are operated by

Central Station from Stationsplein, where you'll find the tourist office (VVV)

Connexxion (www.connexxion.nl). The **national train operator** is Nederlandse Spoorwegen (NS), whose website (www.ns.nl) also has an easy-to-use journey planner which lists departure/ arrival times, fares and platform numbers.

Train timetables are also posted on yellow boards inside Central Station, while upcoming departures appear on digital screens. Generally speaking, trams, metros and ferries (across the IJ to Amsterdam North) run so frequently from around 6am to midnight that you can just turn up and shouldn't have to wait more than a few minutes.

Perhaps most useful of all, especially if your journey involves several types of public transport, is www.9292ov.nl. Type in your nearest public transport stop, train station or even your street address, followed by the location or attraction you want to get to and your preferred time of departure or arrival, and you will be given detailed door-to-door travel advice. You can also view earlier or later departure times and plan your return journey.

ON ARRIVAL
Local transport tickets and passes

Amsterdam has only one airport, Schiphol, located a mere 18km/11mi from the city centre. The airport is on the main railway line between Amsterdam and several cities to the south, including The Hague and Rotterdam, and so is very well serviced. Trains to Central Station (CS), Amsterdam's main public transport hub, run every 10 to 15 minutes throughout the day and the journey takes around 20 minutes.

In 2010, most paper tickets were phased out, to be replaced by the *OV-chipkaart*, a plastic card that allows travel on all public transport *anywhere in the Netherlands*. As a visitor planning to travel within and outside of Amsterdam, your best bet is to **buy an anonymous** *chipkaart* on arrival. These are available for a one-off fee of €7.50 (valid for five years) from NS and GVB machines and service desks. Once you have the card, you will need to put credit onto it. At Schiphol and Central Station you can do this at the yellow and blue machines with coins and credit cards; GVB machines also accept notes (try to avoid all the service desks/information counters at Central Station if you can, as they are invariably busy).

For unlimited travel *within Amsterdam* on bus, tram and metro, you can buy **travel passes** from 24 hours (€7) up to one week (€29). Whatever mode of transport you use, always remember to 'touch in' and 'touch out' at the pink card readers. On trains, you only need to do this at the start and end of your journey. If you take the tram, for example, then change onto the metro to reach your destination, you have to check in and out for each stage of your trip. The card readers will automatically deduct the correct fare.

Tourist information

The main **tourist information office (VVV)** is located on Stationsplein in front of Central Station. It is open daily from 09.00-18.00. This is where you can buy maps, tickets for tours, tourist passes (such as the 'I Amsterdam card'; see www.iamsterdam.com for details of the benefits it offers) or find accommodation if you haven't already done so. The office sells *Time Out Amsterdam*, an English-language magazine published monthly with details of what's on. Queues and waiting times are often long, so unless you are looking for something specific, I hope that *Walk & Eat Amsterdam* will provide all the information you need during your stay!

Shopping for self-catering

Apartments/aparthotels should, as a minimum, have good-quality kitchenettes with two-ring electric burners, a good-sized oven and tea- and coffee-making facilities. There should also be a decent selection of crockery, cutlery and cooking utensils, but you may want to take a few of your own things. What and how much you take will obviously depend on whether you travel by air or not and how much space you have in your luggage.

It is worth thinking about **everyday items** before you go. Basics such as salt and sugar usually only come in large packs and although not expensive, it seems a waste to buy things like this for just a few spoonfuls' use. If your stay is short you might want to bring some of these with you in small containers or bags. The same goes for general daily items such as shampoos and cleaning cloths, which nearly always come in bulk. A bottle of travel wash for laundry is also a good investment.

Your first stop after you arrive will probably be a local **supermarket** to stock up on essentials. The main supermarket chain in the centre of Amsterdam is Albert Heijn and so ubiquitous that you probably won't ever be more than a few minutes' walk from a branch. You can check exact locations on www.ah.nl. Click on 'Winkels'

Supermarket shopping list

salt and pepper
herbs and spices
milk/cream
yoghurt
butter/margarine
eggs
sugar
bread
coffee/tea/drinking chocolate
fruit juice/cordial
soft drinks
wine/beer
cooking oil
salad oil and vinegar
tomato purée
rice/pasta
mayonnaise/mustard /condiments
washing-up liquid or dishwasher tablets
paper towels
soap/shampoo
tissues/toilet paper
scouring pads
cleaning cloths
travel wash
general purpose cleaner

at the top of the homepage and type 'Amsterdam' into the 'uw woonplaats' box or, if you know it, the postcode of your accommodation into the 'uw postcode' box. You can then navigate around the Google Map to find the store closest to you. Click on that store to bring up the opening times. The majority of branches are open for at least a few hours on Sunday, and the larger ones are open 08.00-22.00. Many also have a bakery, a delicatessen counter and a beer and wine aisle, making them a good option if you have missed the local market (see the following section). Other supermarket chains to look out for are Dirk van den Broek, Super de Boer and C1000.

If you are interested in eating **organic** or need to buy **dairy- or gluten-free** products, it is worth investigating Natuurwinkel (www.natuurwinkel.nl), a growing chain of wholefood super-markets. There are branches on or close to several of the walks. See 'Eat GF, DF' on page 138 for more information.

In some supermarkets you are required to weigh your own fruit and vegetables. To do this, put the items on the scales provided and press the button showing the corresponding picture or number (usually displayed on the shelf next to the item). Hit the 'bon' or receipt button and put the barcoded sticker that is printed out on your item for scanning at checkout.

Markets

The biggest and most visited market in the centre is **Albert Cuyp** in De Pijp (Walk 7), which is open every day except Sunday from 09.00-17.00. It isn't exclusively a food market — bike locks, toiletries, cheap clothing and the like are also

Fish stall at Albert Cuyp market (top; Walk 7) and a selection of liqueurs to be sampled at Proeflokaal De Admiraal (Walk 1; see page 31).

A number of stalls at Albert Cuyp market also sell ready-prepared food to eat on the street; see page 82 for suggestions of a couple of treats you might try.

De Admiraal is a 'tasting house', where you can sample several different drinks, served in small glasses. There are many tasting houses in the city, where you can try liqueurs, jenevers and beers; see 'Dutch bar culture and etiquette' on page 24.

available — but you will find a good selection of fresh fruit and vegetables, herbs, cheese, fish, meat, nuts and dried fruit. It can get crushingly busy here on Saturdays, but if you aren't in a hurry it's a lively place to wander.

A growing interest in healthy eating over the last few years has seen an increase in the number of **organic markets**. The oldest, but also the priciest, is the farmers' market on **Noordermarkt** in front of Noorderkerk (Walk 1). Smaller and less crowded is the market on **Nieuwmarkt** (Walk 4). Both are open all day every Saturday. The newest of the bunch, and open on Wednesdays (which is handy if you are visiting during the week), is the market on **Haarlemmerplein** (Walk 6).

The quality of the produce — bread, cheese, meat, fruit and veg, but also home-made preserves and specialty items such as salt and olive oil — is extremely high, and the people running the stalls are usually also the producers. This means they are proud of what they sell and are happy to answer questions or give you a free sample if you can't decide what to buy. All these markets are outside, so wrap up if you plan on visiting them in winter.

Introduction to Dutch cuisine

Dutch food has long had the unfortunate reputation of being bland and stodgy. While it is true that the Netherlands' farming history, coupled with a thrifty Calvinist mentality that has held sway since the 17th century, has meant that simple, sustaining meals have been the norm for the past few centuries, there is much more to Dutch cuisine than meat and potatoes.

The country is extremely fertile, and produces carrots, onions, cauliflowers, beans, apples and other fruit and vegetable crops in abundance. The flat pastures are also ideal for herds of cows, whose milk is used in drinks, yoghurt, a plethora of dairy-based desserts, butter and **cheese**. Gouda is probably the best known overseas, but a visit to any Dutch delicatessen will make it immediately clear that it is not the only cheese on the block. Look out for crumbly old cheeses, smoked cheeses and cheeses flavoured with spices including Leyden, containing cumin seeds, and the aromatic Friese Nagelkaas, made with cloves. Goat's cheese is also gaining in popularity.

The long North Sea coastline is a rich source of **fish and seafood**. **Meat,** in particular pork, chicken and beef, is consumed with gusto at mealtimes, but is also worked into a wide variety of **snacks**. These include croquettes, *bitterballen* (a type of round croquette filled with ragout) and *vlammetjes* (spicy minced meat wrapped in pastry). These, along with Indonesian *loempia's* (spring rolls) and cheese straws are widely available in bars and cafés as *borrelhapjes* (literally small bites to accompany an alcoholic drink).

Having said this, a growing awareness of the environmental impact of meat production and consideration for non-meat eaters mean that **vegetarians** have an increasing number of options. It is very unlikely that you will find yourself in a restaurant with no vegetarian dishes on the menu at all, although it may be assumed that you eat fish.

The Dutch generally eat three meals a day. **Breakfast** usually consists of yoghurt with muesli/cruesli (crunchy muesli comparable to granola), bread topped with cheese, ham or *hagelslag* (chocolate sprinkles) or *ontbijtkoek*, a moist ginger-bread. It is not common to eat toast or cooked food for breakfast at home, particularly during the week, although if you start the day in a café, the breakfast options will often include egg dishes, such as omelettes, scrambled eggs and *uitsmijters* (eggs fried with or without ham, topped with cheese and served on slices of bread).

Lunch is quite a basic affair and predominantly comprises sandwiches and sometimes soup or salad. In many offices, the staff stops work to eat lunch together, often quite early by British standards (around midday). Unlike the UK, where milk is generally regarded as something for children, it is not unusual to see Dutch adults knocking back a glass of milk or two with their sandwiches. **Dinner** is the main meal of the day and is eaten at home between about six and eight o'clock. Eating out is still considered something of a luxury, but Amsterdam has a lively restaurant scene, and there are enough options to suit all budgets.

Alongside milk, the other great lubricant of Dutch society is **coffee**. After Scandinavia, the Netherlands has the highest coffee consumption rate in the world. It is drunk as a stimulant but also has a very social function. It is the beverage of choice at birthday parties (at least until it is deemed appropriate to bring out the alcohol), and nearly every bar and pub has a coffee machine. As a result, the quality of coffee served is generally high, and it is readily available. Traditionally, coffee is served strong and black or with a drop of *koffiemelk,* a kind of condensed milk. Nowadays, a wide range of coffees is served, but the Dutch term for a latte has remained *koffie verkeerd* or 'wrong coffee'. This is allegedly because it is made with more milk than coffee, a ratio deemed strange.

Black and herb **tea** is also popular. If you order tea in a café it is normal to receive a cup of hot water with the tea bag on the side or a basket containing a mix of different teas from which to choose. But you're likely to have to ask for milk if you want it!

Seasonal foods

Like the majority of Western European countries, Dutch supermarkets are well stocked with imported produce that is available year round. Certain local items, however, are only eaten in season and their arrival is highly anticipated. In late

Dutch bar culture and etiquette

The Netherlands is a resolutely beer-drinking country (Dutch brewing conglomerates like Heineken, Grolsch and Amstel are known the world over), although interest in wine is growing. Going for a pint in Amsterdam can be quite different from what you are used to at home, however, so here are some pointers to Dutch drinking culture and etiquette.

For starters, you probably won't see a pint for the duration of your stay, unless you go to an Irish pub. This is because most beer is served as a *vaasje*, comparable to a half pint. Slightly less ubiquitous but still regularly consumed is the *fluitje*, a tiny glass containing little more than a few sips. It does not necessarily follow that the Dutch drink less than other nationalities, but beer is served cold and the advantage of these smaller glasses is that their contents have little chance to warm up before you get to the bottom of them.

Don't be surprised if the beer arrives with a thick head. This is not an industry trick to give punters less than they paid for. About three centimetres of foam is deemed perfect — an indication that the beer is not flat and adds to the creamy sensation when the drink is consumed.

One of the nicest places to sample Dutch beer — either a mainstream pils or one of the more specialised dark or seasonal varieties — is a *bruin café* (brown café). These are traditional watering holes, which get their name

May/early June the first herrings arrive in fishmongers and street-side stalls, accompanied around the same time by asparagus. White asparagus, in particular, is considered a delicacy and is often served simply with sliced ham, eggs and melted butter.

Although the weather is often grey and chilly in the winter, this is made up for by the large number of foods available specifically at this time of year. Pea soup, *stamppot* (mash; see page 115) and game are eaten throughout the cold months,

In De Waag (Walk 4)

from their usually dark interiors and walls stained with years' worth of cigarette smoke. 't Arendsnest (Walk 1) stocks over 100 Dutch-brewed and seasonal beers, while 't Smalle (Walk 2) is housed in a former distillery and serves up plenty of history and charm with its selection of beers and *jenever* (gin flavoured with juniper berries).

Table service in bars is the rule rather than the exception. Your server will automatically open a tab for you, which you settle when you leave. The only time this does not apply is on particularly busy occasions like New Year's Eve and on some large terraces. Visitors to Amsterdam are often surprised by the slow, often disinterested service. Even so, it is common practice to tip the bar staff, as you would waiters in a restaurant. A drink costing €2.80, for example, would usually be rounded up to €3, but 5 percent of the total bill is a good rule of thumb. *Proost!*

while other foods are linked to particular festivals. Around Sinterklaas (Saint Nicholas on 5 December, when gifts are exchanged) shelves fill with chocolate letters, *speculaas* (crunchy spiced biscuits) and *pepernoten* (ginger nuts). As Christmas approaches, these are replaced with *kerstkransen* (almond pastry rings) and *kerststollen* (currant cakes filled with marzipan). *Oliebollen* (deep-fried doughnut balls covered in icing sugar) and *appelflappen* (apple turnovers) are associated with New Year's Eve, but stalls set up all over town several weeks before that.

Starting at the floating Flower Market and proceeding to the elegant canal-side houses built by the city's wealthy residents during the Netherlands' Golden Age, this walk gives a taste of life in the very centre of Amsterdam.

central canals

WALK

Start at Munttoren (1), the
tower on the corner of Rokin
and Muntplein. At the base of
the tower, which dates from
the 15th century and formed
part of the city walls, is the
floating **Flower Market (2)**.
Flowers play an important
role in the Dutch economy,
and although the real action
takes place at the Flower
Auction in Aalsmeer (close to
Schiphol Airport), the Flower
Market is still a colourful
place to wander or pick up a
packet of bulbs to take home.
At the end of the market turn
left onto Koningsplein and at
Keizersgracht turn right.

**See map on the inside front
cover**
Distance: 5km/3mi; 1h30min
Grade: easy; on well-maintained
paths throughout and walkable all
year round
Equipment: see pages 12-13; sun
protection
Transport: 🚋 4, 9, 14, 16, 24 or
25 to Muntplein; return from Rokin on
the same trams
Refreshments: numerous cafés
and restaurants en route; Gartine for
breakfast, lunch or high tea;
Proeflokaal De Admiraal for drinks
and/or dinner
Points of interest
Flower Market
Nine Streets
Westerkerk
Anne Frank House
Noordermarkt

Keizersgracht (Emperor's
Canal) is the second canal — between Herengracht (Gentle-
men's Canal) and Prinsengracht (Prince's Canal) — in the string
of canals that forms a horseshoe around Amsterdam's medieval
centre. Construction on this western section of the horseshoe
began in 1613 and was home to the city's wealthy residents. To
get an impression of the size of these houses, which often
extend far back from the street, stop in at **Huis Marseille (3)** at
number 401. Built by a French merchant in 1665 (there is a stone

tablet showing a map of the harbour at Marseilles on the facade), the house is now a photography museum (admission €5, children up to 17 free, www.huismarseille.nl).

At the junction with Huidenstraat, turn left over the canal and onto Runstraat. This is one of the **'Nine Streets'**, the collective name given to the nine narrow, boutique-filled streets between Leidsegracht to the south and Raadhuisstraat to the north that link the main canals. Look out for De Kaaskamer (number 7), a shop you'll smell before you see, selling an impressive range of Dutch and European cheeses, and Paul Année organic bakery (number 25). Both are good places for picking up (picnic) supplies.

At Prinsengracht, turn right and walk along the canal to **Westerkerk** (West Church; **4**). Designed by architect Hendrick de Keyser and opened in 1631, this Protestant church boasts an 85-metre tower topped with the imperial crown of Emperor Maximilian I. The tower itself is climbable and affords a magnificent view of the city (tours every 30min Apr-Sept Mon-Sat 10.00-17.30; Oct Mon-Sat 11.00-16.00; €6). The painter Rembrandt was buried here in 1669.

Pass the **Anne Frank House (5)**, where Anne wrote her famous diary while hiding from the Nazis, and at the next

Westerkerk

canal, Leliegracht, turn left over the bridge, then right up the western side of Prinsengracht. Walk straight up to **Noorderkerk** (North Church; **6**), another Protestant church, this one built for the poor living in the neighbouring Jordaan (Walk 2). **Noordermarkt,** the square in front of the church, hosts a flea market on Mondays and an organic farmers' market on Saturdays.

At the end of Prinsengracht you can make a small detour to visit the peaceful internal gardens of two 17th-century *hofjes* (almshouses). To do so, turn left onto Brouwersgracht and take the first left onto Lindengracht. **Lindenhofje** is at number 94 and **Suyckerhofje** at 149. The gardens are intended for use by the residents of the houses

Gardens at Suyckerhofje

surrounding them, but when the doors are unlocked visitors are welcome to have a peek. Retrace your steps to get back to the end of Prinsengracht. Turn right onto Brouwersgracht and right again at the end of it onto Herengracht. If you're in need of liquid refreshment at this point, stop at **'t Arendsnest** (number 90; **7**), a bar that stocks more than 100 Dutch-brewed beers, plus seasonal beers such as *bockbier* which is served in the autumn.

Continue down the canal, looking out for the ornate **Bartolotti House** (number 170, shown on page 26), also thought to be the work of Hendrick de Keyser. When you reach the crossing with Wolvenstraat, turn left over Herengracht. **De Admiraal** (**8**; see opposite) is just off to the right. Continue straight ahead along Oude Spiegelstraat to Singel. Walk right along Singel until it meets Koningsplein. Cross the tram tracks but, instead of going back down the Flower Market, turn left and head down narrow Heiligeweg. At the end of Heiligeweg, turn left onto **Kalverstraat**, Amsterdam's main shopping street. Cross Spui (Waterstone's bookshop is on the corner), and take the first alley, Taksteeg, on your right. This is where you'll find **Gartine (9)**, a delightful café (see page 32). At the end of Taksteeg is **Rokin**, with trams to your final destination.

Proeflokaal De Admiraal

This atmospheric bar and restaurant is located in what was once a distillery. Many traces of the distillery are still in evidence, from the copper distilling kettles in the corners to the shelves lined with wooden barrels. Even the toilets are located inside enormous 10,000-litre vats!

It is appropriate, then, that this *proeflokaal* (tasting house) should be linked to A van Wees, the last remaining distillery in the centre of Amsterdam. The bar is well stocked with traditional *jenevers* (Dutch gins) and liqueurs (see photograph on page 20). The idea of a tasting house is, as the name suggests, that you can sample several different drinks. A selection of gins or liqueurs is served in small glasses, allowing you to sip and compare each one. Enjoy them with a plate of snacks at the bar or settle into one of the many dark corners for a no-nonsense Dutch meal. There is also a wine list — scribbled on the barrels above the bar — if hard liquor isn't your thing.

PROEFLOKAAL DE ADMIRAAL
Herengracht 319
(020 625 4334
www.proeflokaaldeadmiraal.nl
Open: Mon-Fri 16.30-01.00; Sat 17.00-01.00 €€

menu comprises hearty portions of solid Dutch dishes

starters include a mixed fish plate of North Sea shrimp, smoked eel and salmon, served with toast

mains are based on meat and fish — steak with mushroom sauce, halibut with mustard sauce — accompanied by potatoes and crispy vegetables. **Limited vegetarian options**

desserts include ice cream and Dutch apple pie

Gartine

In a narrow alley off Kalver-straat, the main shopping street, tiny Gartine conjures up superlative breakfasts, lunches and high teas in its even tinier kitchen. The café is run by a passionate couple who grow a lot of the fruit, vegetables and herbs used in the restaurant in their own garden and orchard. Gartine has limited seating, but is well worth getting up early for, or reserve a table if you plan on visiting later in the day.

> **GARTINE**
> Taksteeg 7 (020 320 4132
> www.gartine.nl
> **Open: Wed-Sun** 10.00–18.00 €-€€
>
> **menu** combines Dutch and southern European dishes
>
> **breakfast** options include toasted nut bread with Gouda cheese, and chocolate brioche served with butter and lemon curd
>
> **lunchtime sandwiches** made with inventive fillings — blue cheese and rhubarb chutney, smoked sausage with piccalilli mayonnaise, bacon with cream of Dijon mustard and marinated radishes
>
> **high tea** served from 14.00

The breakfast recipe opposite comes from Gartine: it's French toast, known as *wentelteefjes* (pronounced **ven**-tel-tay-fias) in Dutch. There is much speculation about the origins of this rather odd word, but the theory most often cited is that it is a contraction of *wentel het eventjes* or 'turn it briefly'. This refers to one of the final steps in preparation, when slices of bread are dipped and turned in a milk mixture until coated on both sides.

Sugar bread is a luxurious sweet bread prepared with whole sugar cubes. It can be found in Dutch bakeries and larger supermarkets. Or make your own with the recipe from Hartog's bakery on page 104.

restaurants

eat

Sugar bread French toast with apple-cinnamon butter

For the 'butter', bring the cider to the boil in a large saucepan. On a low heat, reduce to half its original volume. Grate the lemon rind, halve the lemon and extract the juice.

Add the apples, lemon rind, lemon juice and cinnamon to the cider. Mix well and cook gently for 10 minutes with the lid on. Remove the lid and cook for a further 20-25 minutes, until the apples are soft. Stir occasionally to prevent sticking.

Take the mixture off the heat and leave to cool for 10 minutes. In a food processor, blend in small amounts until smooth. Measure the mixture and add 100 g sugar per 300 ml. Return the mixture to a low heat, stir until the sugar has dissolved and cook for a final 20 minutes, to achieve a creamy 'butter'.

To make the milk mixture, grate the lemon rind and combine with the sugar, cinnamon, egg and salt in a large, shallow bowl. Gradually whisk in the milk.

Heat the butter in a frying pan and cut eight thick slices of sugar bread. Dip each slice briefly in the milk mixture, turn and coat the other side. Shake off any excess mixture and fry in the butter until golden brown (2-3 minutes on each side).

Serve warm, generously spread with the apple-cinnamon butter.

Ingredients (for 4 people)

250 ml dry cider
450 g tart apples, peeled, cored, cut into chunks
1 lemon
1/2 tsp ground cinnamon
approx 100 g sugar

For the milk mixture

1 lemon
25 g sugar
1/2 tsp ground cinnamon
1 egg
pinch of salt
200 ml milk
1 loaf sugar bread
2 tbsp butter

recipes

eat

Just west of the centre, the Jordaan used to be a working-class neighbourhood. Although this is no longer the case, cosy 'brown cafés' and narrow, higgledy-piggledy streets hint at a less affluent past. This zigzag walk takes in the area's most popular canals, as well as its quiet residential backwaters.

jordaan

WALK

Start this walk at **Leidse-plein**. Facing the grand **Stads-schouwburg** theatre **(10)**, walk down the right-hand side of it onto Lijnbaans-gracht. You will pass **Melk-weg** on your left, once a dairy (the name translates as 'Milky Way') and now one of Amsterdam's main music and cultural venues. Cross the bridge and carry on along Lijnbaansgracht until you reach Elandsgracht. As the name suggests, this was once a *gracht* (canal), but has been filled in and is now a popular shopping street. Turn right

See map on the inside front cover
Distance: 5km/3mi; 1h30min
Grade: easy; on well-maintained paths throughout and walkable all year round
Equipment: see pages 12-13; sun protection
Transport: 🚋 1, 2, 5, 7 or 10 to Leidseplein. Return on trams or metros from Central Station
Refreshments: numerous cafés and restaurants en route; Small World Catering and Pancakes!
Points of interest
Stadsschouwburg theatre
De Drie Hendricken
Brouwersgracht
Haarlemmerdijk

here. About halfway down Elandsgracht, turn left onto **Hazen-straat** (but to get to **Pancakes! (11)**, the restaurant recommended on page 40, walk to the end of Elandsgracht and cross the canal to Berenstraat). Hazenstraat is a lovely little street full of art galleries and bric-a-brac and vintage clothing shops. It changes its name several times (Tweede Lauriersdwarsstraat, Tweede Rozendwarsstraat and Akoleienstraat) before it ends on Bloemstraat.

Turn right onto Bloemstraat, take the first left onto Tweede Bloemdwarsstraat and, at the canal (Bloemgracht), turn right.

Look up at the corner building (number 51), which has a female torso built into the facade. **De Drie Hendricken** is the trio of houses at numbers 87, 89, 91. Dating from 1642 they have beautiful, and now relatively rare, step-gables. Above the lintel are three reliefs depicting the Townsman, the Countryman and the Seaman, a reference to the old house names. Almost opposite them is the red-brick **Restored Apostolic Mission Church (12)**.

Take the first bridge left over the canal and onto Tweede Leliedwarsstraat. Walk up to Egelantiersgracht. Cross over the bridge, turn right and walk down the other side of the canal. Then take the first left down Tweede Egelantiersdwarsstraat. (But if you would like to experience a traditional 'brown café', first carry along Egelantiersgracht to **'t Smalle (13)** at number 12. The history of this charming bar, with a lovely canal-side terrace, goes back to 1780 when the Hoppe distillery was established here. The pictures in the stained-glass windows still hark back to those early days. Alongside beer, wine and *jenever* (Dutch gin), in the winter you can also warm up over a glass of *glühwein* (mulled wine). Retrace your steps to Tweede Egelantiersdwarsstraat to continue the walk.)

Follow Tweede Egelantiersdwarsstraat to Westerstraat, where a **clothing and textile market** is held every Monday. Cross over Westerstraat and turn right; then take the first left onto Tweede Boomdwarsstraat. Opposite the children's playground turn right onto Lindenstraat and take the first left onto Eerste Lindendwarsstraat.

Walk straight on until you reach Willemsstraat and turn

right. The canal at the end of Willemsstraat is **Brouwersgracht**, arguably the most picturesque in Amsterdam. Just on the other side of the green bridge is a former brewery (numbers 204-206, one of several that gave this canal its name) and the 'Small Green Deer' warehouse — you can see the eponymous animals standing watch on the roof. Cross the bridge and turn immediately left to walk down the northern side of Brouwersgracht. The canal is lined with old warehouses, the majority of which have been carefully renovated and turned into desirable apartments and office spaces.

At the end of Brouwersgracht turn right onto Korte Marnixstraat and right again at the traffic lights. Walk round Haarlemmerplein, and turn right onto **Haarlemmerdijk**, another bustling shopping street, mostly lined with boutiques

Old houses on Egelantiersgracht

and independent outlets. A few doors up is The Movies, an art-house cinema with a gorgeous art deco interior, and at number 71 is Teabar, a specialist shop selling around 60 kinds of loose tea from transparent plastic bins. Four streets down on the right is Binnen Oranjestraat where you'll find **Small World Catering** (**14**; see below).

Haarlemmerdijk becomes Haarlemmerstraat. At the end of the street, cross Singel canal and you will see the train tracks leading into **Central Station** on the left. To get there turn left onto the main road, Prins Hendrikkade, and follow it to the right for about 300m/yds for public transport to your final destination.

Small World Catering

Small by name and small by nature, this tiny café and deli nonetheless pumps out large portions of home-made pies and quiches, well-filled sand-wiches and chunks of fabulous cakes. In warm weather a few extra chairs are set up on the pavement outside, and there is a take-away counter if you want to pack a picnic.

SMALL WORLD CATERING
Binnen Oranjestraat 14
(**020 420 2774**
www.smallworldcatering.nl
Open: Tue-Sat 10.30-20.00; Sun noon-20.00 €

menu with a strong global flavour wide selection of **sandwiches**, made with focaccia, ciabatta or brown bread, with fillings including pastrami, Ementaler and coleslaw, and fresh tuna with red caper tapenade

quiches, pasta salad and **couscous** also available

sweets include muffins, brownies, lemon tart and carrot cake

restaurants

eat

Pancakes!

Although the name of this bustling restaurant on one of the narrow 'Nine Streets' won't leave you in any doubt as to its speciality, this is a pancake house with a difference. Alongside Dutch pancakes topped with well-loved combinations like ham and cheese and bacon and apple, there are also *drie in de pan* (three in the pan), a trio of mini pancakes, and *poffertjes*, a mound of even tinier pancakes served with sugar and butter (see photograph on page 84).

The menu also roams beyond the Dutch borders, to include French *galettes*, American pancakes served with maple syrup, and Chinese pancakes stuffed with chicken, spring onions, ginger and herbs.

Gluten-free pancakes (buckwheat/rice flour batter) are available.

PANCAKES!
Berenstraat 38
(020 528 9797
www.pancakesamsterdam.nl
Open: daily 10.00-19.00 €

menu featuring both Dutch and global pancakes

3 child-sized pancakes

choice of **breakfast pancakes**, both sweet and savoury, including a muesli pancake

12 Dutch and **9 Dutch deluxe pancakes** — like the unusual chicory, ham and camembert pancake with raspberry sauce

restaurants

eat

Pancakes with spinach and goat's cheese

This recipe comes from Pancakes! To make the pancake batter, sift the flour in a bowl and add the sugar and salt. Make a well in the flour and pour in the milk and eggs. Beat to a smooth batter.

Put a tablespoon of oil in a large frying pan and heat over a medium flame. When the oil is hot, cover the bottom of the frying pan with spinach (about 200 g per pancake — it will shrink considerably when cooked) and cover with three or four ladles of batter. Swirl the batter around so that the spinach and the bottom of the pan are covered.

When the top of the pancake is almost dry, flip it over and crumble a slice of goat's cheese evenly across the surface. Turn down the heat and let the cheese melt (you may want to put a lid on the pan), about 3-4 minutes.

Slide the pancake carefully onto a plate and garnish with pine nuts and a few drops of garlic oil. Serve immediately. Repeat for the other pancakes, adding more oil to the frying pan as necessary.

Ingredients (for around 8 large pancakes)

500 g self-raising white flour
2 tbsp sugar
2 tsp salt
1 l milk
2 medium eggs
sunflower oil for frying

For the topping

1.5 kg fresh spinach, stalks removed
160 g soft goat's cheese
pine nuts and garlic oil to garnish

recipes

eat

This walk weaves through the Old Centre, home to an extraordinary number of centuries-old churches and houses, as well as the Red Light District and Chinatown. The walk then continues on to the adjoining Jewish Quarter, taking in Rembrandt's house and the Auschwitz memorial in pretty Wertheimpark.

old centre & jewish quarter

WALK

3

This **walk starts** on the
western side of **Stationsplein**,
the square in front of Central
Station where trams from the
south and west terminate.
Follow Damrak, the road running south from the station;
this is one of the first things
that visitors to Amsterdam see
when they get off the train.
Lined with tacky souvenir
shops and cafés of question-
able quality, it does offer a few
points of interest, however,
and soon leads to much more
picturesque parts of town.

About halfway down
Damrak, on the left, is the

See map on the inside front cover

Distance: 5.5km/3.4mi; 1h45min

Grade: easy; on well-maintained paths throughout and walkable all year round

Equipment: see pages 12-13; sun protection

Transport: any 🚋, metro or 🚌 to Central Station. Return on 🚋 4, 9, 14, 16, 24 or 25 from Rokin

Refreshments: numerous cafés and restaurants en route, including Café Latei (featured)

Points of interest
Royal Palace
Red Light District
Oude Kerk
Jewish Quarter
Waterlooplein Market

(predominantly) red-brick **Beurs van Berlage (15)**. Designed by
architect Hendrik Petrus Berlage, the building was opened in
1903 as the stock exchange. The exchange quickly outgrew the
premises and relocated across the square, and the Beurs is now
used for concerts and events. One of these is the Bokbierfestival,
the Netherlands' largest beer festival, held annually at the end
of October. The architectural style of the building was quite
revolutionary for the time and paved the way for the
Amsterdam School. Just one example is the statues on three
corners of the exterior, all of which are nestled in and flush with

Statue on a corner of the Beurs building

the façade. This is in contrast to other buildings from the same era, such as Central Station and the Rijksmuseum, where statues and other decorations were designed to stand out, literally and metaphorically.

At the end of Damrak is **Dam Square**, a large expanse of concrete bounded on the west by the **Royal Palace** and on the east by the **National Monument (16)**, a 72-foot obelisk commemorating the Dutch victims of war. The palace, which was designed by Jacob van Campen, was originally built in the 17th century as the City Hall. It became the Royal Palace in 1808 shortly after Napoleon had installed his brother Louis as king of the Netherlands. It has been state property since 1936 but is still occasionally used by the Royal Family. At the time of writing the exterior was being cleaned and covered in scaffolding, but the interior was open to the public. Particularly impressive is the Citizens Hall, with a gleaming marble floor depicting maps of the world and the constellations of the northern hemisphere. To the right of the palace is **Nieuwe Kerk** (New Church; **17**), built in the early 15th century for the worshippers who could no longer be accommodated in Oude Kerk (Old Church, passed later in the walk).

Walk round the National Monument and head left down Damstraat. Turn left again at Oudezijds Voorburgwal canal.

Officially part of the **Red Light District** (see photograph on page 56), which occupies a roughly triangular area between Central Station, Dam Square and Nieuwmarkt, this part of the canal is still quite genteel and lined with opulent Golden Age residences.

Prostitution in the Netherlands has been recognised as a legal profession since 1988, and brothels were legalised in 2000. While there are some seedy corners of the Red Light District, it is generally very safe, even at night, and the openness with which the sex trade is conducted is something you should see at least once in your lifetime. This is also the oldest part of the city, which means there are plenty of things to ogle that have nothing to do with the scantily clad ladies in their glowing red windows.

One of these is **Oude Kerk (18)**, a few hundred metres/ yards along Oudezijds Voorburgwal. Founded in the 13th century, it is the oldest church in Amsterdam. Originally Catholic, after the Alteration in 1578 it became Protestant. The interior is suitably austere, but comes alive each spring when the winning entries of the World Press Photo contest are exhibited here before beginning their global tour (church open Mon-Sat 11.00-17.00; Sun 13.00-17.00; normal admission €5 but a supplement of €2.50 is charged for the World Press Photo exhibition; children under 10 free).

Also on Oudezijds Voorburgwal is **Our Lord in the Attic (19)**, an example of a Catholic place of worship. Hidden behind the facade of a typical 17th-century canal house, now **Museum Amstelkring**, this tiny attic church was built during the period

Catholics were forbidden from openly practising their religion. Check www.opsolder.nl for visiting details, as parts of the church and museum were undergoing restoration at the time of writing.

At the end of the canal, turn right onto Sint Olofssteeg and right again onto Zeedijk. As the name suggests, **Zeedijk** was built in the 14th century as a dyke to protect Amsterdam, at that time a swampy fishing village, from the sea. In the 1970s the street had a reputation as an easy place to score drugs. Over the past few decades, however, it has been significantly cleaned up and now forms the centre of Amsterdam's modest **Chinatown**. Unsurprisingly, this is one of the best places to find cheap, tasty Asian food. Nam Kee (number 111) is particularly popular and has even been immortalised by Dutch author Kees van Beijnum who named one of his books, *The Oysters from Nam Kee,* after them. Also on this street is the colourful **He Hua Buddhist temple (20)**.

At the end of Zeedijk is **Café Latei (21**; see page 52) and the back of the imposing **De Waag (22)** that dominates **Nieuwmarkt**. Walk left around the building and admire the turreted bulk of this former weigh house from the front. It is now a restaurant, lit by 300 candles at night (the recommended restaurant for Walk 4; photograph page 54).

With De Waag behind you, walk down Sint Antoniesbreestraat, the road to the left of the Oriental supermarket. You are now in the former **Jewish Quarter**. Just past the crossing with Nieuwe Hoogstraat, you will see a stone archway on your right leading to **Zuiderkerk** (South Church; **23**). Like

Westerkerk (Walk 1) you can climb Zuiderkerk's tower for a look at the carillon (which rings out every 15 minutes) and fantastic views over the eastern side of the city (open Apr-Sept Mon-Sat 13.00-17.00; tours every 30 minutes, adults €6, children, minimum age of 6, €3).

Carry straight on along Jodenbreestraat. Walk left round the Mr Visserplein junction onto Muiderstraat. Take the second left onto Nieuwe Herengracht and admire the street's rich mix of architectural styles, notably the ornate railing and frontage of the 'double house' (it is twice as wide as most canal houses) at number 103.

Turn right over the bridge onto Anne Frankstraat and follow the road to the right past the tennis courts. Cross the road and take the first left onto Henri Polaklaan. At

He Hua Buddhist temple and Zuiderkerk (below)

number 9 is the former headquarters of the **Diamond Workers' Union**, of which Henri Polak was the leader. Also known as The Fortress because of its imposing tower and impenetrable appearance, the building is another example of Hendrik Petrus Berlage's work. It is now the Trade Unions Museum but, unless you have a particular interest in union history, it is more interesting as an architectural landmark than a museum.

Turn right at the end of Henri Polaklaan onto Plantage Kerklaan and walk to the traffic lights. Just on the other side of the lights on the left is **Sagra dell'Uva**. Specialising in Italian wines, mostly self-imported from small wine producers, the emphasis at this excellent wine shop is on top-quality wines at reasonable prices. If you are planning on packing a picnic or are staying in self-catering accommodation, simply tell owner Gennaro Buongiovanni what you are going to eat and how much you want to spend, and he will be happy to recommend a bottle of something that matches your food and budget (open Thur-Fri 12.00-20.00; Sat 11.00-19.00).

If you skip the wine shop, at the traffic lights turn right onto Plantage Middenlaan and cross the road to reach the **Hollandsche Schouwburg** (**24**; open daily 11.00-16.00, free admission). Built in 1892 as a theatre, in 1942 and 1943 it was used by the Nazis as a deportation centre for Jews. It became a war memorial in 1962. A small exhibition upstairs details the persecution of Jews in the Netherlands, while one wall in the chapel downstairs bears the 6700 surnames of the 104,000 Dutch Jews who were exterminated

Further along Plantage Middenlaan is the entrance to

Wertheimpark. In the eastern corner of the park is the **Monument of Mirrors (25)**, which also commemorates the Jews who died during WWII. The park is a peaceful place to take a break and is particularly pretty in spring when it is filled with daffodils and crocuses.

About 50 metres/yards further along on the left is **Hortus Botanicus**. Established in 1638 as a medicinal herb garden, this is one of the oldest botanical gardens in the world. Covering an area of just 1.2 hectares, Hortus Botanicus is home to around 4000 different plant species, as well as an impressive greenhouse divided into subtropical, tropical and desert zones (open Mon-Fri 09.00-17.00; Sat-Sun 10.00-17.00; Jul/Aug daily until 19.00; admission €7.50; children 5-14 €3.50).

Wooden roses of remembrance at Hollandsche Schouwburg

Standing on the same side of the road as the botanical gardens, cross the bridge and follow Muiderstraat back to Mr Visserplein. Walk left round the junction to the 300-year-old **Portuguese Synagogue (26)**. This square colossus has been nicknamed 'the hidden giant' because, despite its size, it seems to go unnoticed by passersby. The fine sand on the floor of the interior is a traditional means of

Greenhouses at Hortus Botanicus

absorbing moisture and dirt and muffling noise — it is not a result of the renovations currently underway in parts of the building (open Apr-Oct Sun-Fri 10.00-16.00; Nov-Mar Sun-Thur 10.00-16.00, Fri 10.00-14.00; www.esnoga.nl; admission €6.50, children over 13 €3.50.). The statue of the dock worker in front of the synagogue commemorates the widespread strikes on 25 February 1941 against Nazi persecution of the Jews.

Continuing left round the junction will take you past the **Jewish Historical Museum (27)** and eventually to **Waterlooplein Market**. The market, which is open every day except Sunday, mostly sells second-hand clothes and bric-a-brac. It is popular with bargain hunters, but is a colourful place to wander even if you have no intention of buying. At the far end of the market turn right and walk up the short flight of steps. On your right is the popular **Rembrandt House (28)**, where the famous artist lived between 1639 and 1658, before the high mortgage payments bankrupted him and he was forced to move. The property and its contents were inventoried for Rembrandt's creditors and these records were used when the house was restored to its original state in the 1990s (open daily 10.00-17.00; www. rembrandthuis.nl; admission €9, children over 6 €2.50).

Cross the bridge and go down the flight of steps on the other side of the canal. Turn left over the next bridge and take the first right onto Raamgracht. Over the following bridge, the road becomes Rusland. Take the first left off Rusland onto Oudezijds Achterburgwal. Turn right at the bridge and walk straight on to **Rokin** for trams onwards.

Rembrandt House (to the left of the bar

Café Latei

Latei is probably Amsterdam's quirkiest café. Located on Zeedijk, which is lined predominantly with Asian restaurants, Latei stands out not only for its very Dutch menu but also for the non-food items it sells. In the cosy, split-level interior, where an arty crowd of regulars rubs shoulders with curious tourists, the walls are lined with everything from second-hand 1970s fondue sets to colourful rolls of wallpaper, while the ceiling drips with retro light fittings. Even the chairs you are sitting on are for sale. Three evenings a week (Thur-Sat) the café dishes up generous portions of Indian food, always with both a meat and vegetarian option.

Open sandwich at Latei, drizzled with organic olive oil

CAFÉ LATEI
Zeedijk 143
(020 625 7485
www.latei.net
Open: Mon-Wed 08.00-18.00; Thur-Fri 08.00-22.00; Sat 09.00-22.00; Sun 11.00-18.00
€ — cash only

compact **menu** of Dutch favourites, made with quality, largely organic ingredients

yoghurt with muesli and *uitsmijters* (fried eggs and ham, sometimes topped with cheese, and served on slices of bread) for **breakfast**

wholesome sandwiches and soup for **lunch**

sweets: excellent apple pie and gooey chocolate cake, washed down with quality coffee or fresh mint tea

restaurants

eat

Huzaren salad

Huzaren salad (pronounced hoo-**zah**-ren) is easy to make, and thus often appears at parties and buffets. It is said to have got its name from the *huzaren* or cavalrymen stationed across the Netherlands several centuries ago. Underfed, they would knock on the kitchen doors of rich households and the maids would give them the cold left-overs of the evening's dinner. This version uses all fresh ingredients!

Ingredients (for 4 people)

1 tbsp white wine vinegar
125 ml crème fraîche
150 g cooked ham, cubed
150 g cooked potatoes, cubed
125 g cooked beetroot, cubed
1 carrot, peeled and cubed
1/2 red apple, cubed
2 medium hard-boiled eggs
4 cocktail gherkins
1 tbsp finely chopped fresh parsley
1 tbsp finely chopped fresh dill
salt and freshly ground black pepper
small head of lettuce

Mix the vinegar and crème fraîche in a large bowl. Stir in the meat, vegetables and apple.

Peel the eggs. Cut one of them into small cubes and slice the other. Slice the gherkins. Mix the cubed egg and gherkins into the salad with the herbs. Season with salt and pepper to taste.

Wash and drain the lettuce leaves. Use enough leaves to line a serving bowl, then heap the salad onto them.

Arrange the egg slices on top. Serve as a side dish or as a light meal with fresh, crusty bread.

recipes

eat

Amsterdam, with its canals, is often referred to as the Venice of the north. All this water results in beautiful reflections, particularly at night when the bridges are lit. This leisurely walk follows the River Amstel to the twinkling Skinny Bridge and ends at the candlelit In De Waag restaurant on Nieuwmarkt.

night walk

WALK

Start the walk at **Weesper-plein**. If you arrive by metro, take the exit marked Sarphati-straat/Amstel. If arriving by tram from the west, you will need to cross the road after you alight. With the metro exit behind you, walk straight ahead along Sarphatistraat, past the ABN Amro bank, towards the **River Amstel**.

Next to the river on the left is the **Amstel Hotel**. Opened in 1867, this grand dame of Amsterdam hotels, shown on page 90, attracted dignitaries almost from the start and is still known today as the favourite haunt of international cele-brities when they are in town. Just before the bridge over the river, turn right onto Amstel.

> **See map on the inside front cover**
> **Distance:** 3km/2mi; 1h
> **Grade:** easy; on well-maintained paths throughout and walkable all year round
> **Equipment:** see pages 12-13
> **Transport:** metro 51, 53 or 54, or 🚊 7 or 10 to Weesperplein; return on metros from Nieuwmarkt
> **Refreshments:** numerous cafés and restaurants en route; dinner at In De Waag
> **Points of interest**
> Royal Carré Theatre
> Magere Brug
> Reguliersgracht
> Europe's narrowest house

The first point of interest on this street is the impressive **Amstelsluizen** spanning the river. These locks, which date from 1674 and are still in use today, allow the canals to be flushed with fresh water several times a week. Opposite them is the **Royal Carré Theatre**, originally built in 1887 by Oscar Carré as a circus. It still hosts a Christmas Circus each year, but is best known for its musical, theatre and dance performances.

A little further along is the beautiful **Magere Brug (29)**

drawbridge. According to popular myth, it is named after the Mager sisters who lived on opposite sides of the

Red Light District (left), 'Skinny' Bridge (Magere Brug) and the Carré Theatre

river and built a wooden bridge to make it easier to visit each other. It is much more likely, however, that the name refers to the bridge's width ('mager' means 'skinny' in Dutch) which, when it was first built, was so narrow that two people could barely cross at the same time. The current bridge is not quite so slim, but the name has stuck.

Cross the bridge, which leads directly to Kerkstraat. Cross Utrechtsestraat and continue on to Amstelveld. On the northwestern corner of this leafy square is the wooden **Amstelkerk** (Amstel Church). It was built between 1668 and 1670 as an emergency place of worship for the residents of the newly laid second stretch of the central canal belt (the first stretch is covered in Walk 1). As it was only intended to be temporary, the design was so simple that it was

termed a 'preekschuur' (literally a sermon shed). Plans for a permanent brick church on this site were never realised and the 'shed' is now used for concerts, theatre performances and events.

Turn right after the church onto **Reguliersgracht**. The spot where it crosses Herengracht is perhaps one of the most photographed in the city because it offers a view of seven old bridges, their arches beautifully lit at night with small white lights.

Continue straight on to **Rembrandtplein** — this is a busy square surrounded by several bars and restaurants, but offers little of interest to discerning diners. Then go down Halvemaansteeg, the small alley directly in front of you. This will bring you back onto Amstel. Cross the road to the waterfront side and turn left. The street becomes Rokin and, just past Reederij P Kooij tour boat company, the river goes underground. Turn right here and then take the first left on to narrow **Nes**. This was the centre of the tobacco trade in the 19th century, but since the 1960s the street has been the centre of Amsterdam's theatre land, with no less than five theatres along its short length.

At Dam Square, turn right onto Damstraat. Where this street becomes Oude Hoogstraat, look out for the house at number 22. At just 2.02 metres/6.5ft wide, it is said to be the **narrowest house in Europe**. Turn left at Kloveniersburgwal and walk to Nieuwmarkt. In the centre of the square is **De Waag**. The eye-catching building has had several incarnations, but is now a café and restaurant where you can dine by candlelight (see pages 25, 54 and overleaf).

In De Waag

The history of the imposing building in the centre of Nieuwmarkt (see photographs on page 25 and 54) goes back to 1488. It was originally built as one of the three gatehouses for the city's defences, which explains its sturdy, castle-like appearance. The city walls were demolished in 1601 to make way for urban expansion and the building lost its original function. In 1617 it became a weigh house and was also used by various guilds. One of these was the Surgeons' Guild, who performed (very popular) public dissections. This rather unappetising practice disappeared along with the guilds in the early 19th century, and for the next 150 years or so the building was used variously as a furniture factory, fire station and museum.

IN DE WAAG
Nieuwmarkt 4
(020 422 7772
www.indewaag.nl
Open: daily for lunch 10.00-16.00 and dinner 17.00-22.30 €€

Dutch/Mediterranean **menu** that changes with the seasons

starters include cream of parsnip soup with blue cheese; smoked salmon and asparagus salad with avocado mousse

mains — beef, chicken and fish options, but vegetarians are also well-catered for with dishes such as smoked pumpkin stuffed with potatoes and vegetables, and polenta with thyme and lemon zest, served with blue cheese sauce

both sweet and savoury **dessert** options: warm chocolate cake, stewed pears, assorted Dutch cheeses

impressive selection of **wine** served by the glass (each item on the menu is followed by a wine suggestion)

It has been a café and restaurant since 1995. The interior, with stone floor, thick walls and few windows, retains an authentic feel — enhanced by 300 candles that provide night-time illumination.

restaurants

eat

Mustard soup

Mustard is a popular ingredient in dressings, sauces and, as in this example, soups. The idea can take a little getting used to, but the taste is tangy and delicious.

Slice the leeks into rings. Heat the oil in a large, heavy-bottomed pan on a low flame and cook the leeks until soft, but not brown, about 4-5 minutes. Stir regularly. Add the yellow mustard and mix well.

Add the stock and potatoes, bring to the boil and simmer for 20 minutes, or until the potatoes are soft.

While the soup is simmering, fry the bacon with a teaspoon of sunflower oil until light brown and crispy. Drain on a piece of kitchen towel.

Puree the soup carefully in the pan with a handheld blender and bring to the boil once again.

On a low heat, add the crème fraîche and cheese and stir until melted.

Add the course mustard and bacon. Season with salt and pepper to taste. Divide the soup between four bowls and serve with slices of fresh, crusty bread.

Ingredients (for 4 people)

1 tbsp sunflower oil
2 leeks
2 tbsp yellow mustard (such as Dijon)
2 small potatoes, peeled and diced
100 g bacon, cubed
750 ml vegetable stock
150 ml (low-fat) crème fraîche
100 g cheese, grated
3 tbsp coarse mustard (containing seeds)
salt and freshly ground black pepper

recipes

eat

Forming a loop, the theme of this walk is water and Amsterdam's maritime history. Starting and ending at Central Station, it takes in the glass-fronted buildings on the IJ, the modern residential Java and KNSM islands and the old warehouses where goods arriving in the city by boat were once stored.

zeeburg & the eastern islands

WALK

Start the walk at **Central Station**: walk all the way through the station building to the back exit that gives on to the **IJ**, the stretch of water that separates the city centre from Amsterdam North. Cross over to the waterfront side of the road and turn right. On your left, as the road starts to incline, is the glass-fronted **Muziekgebouw aan 't IJ** cultural centre, opened in 2005. As well as hosting a full

Distance: 7km/4.3mi; 2h

Grade: easy; on well-maintained paths throughout and walkable all year round

Equipment: see pages 12-13; sun protection

Transport: any 🚃, metro or 🚌 to Central Station; return the same way

Refreshments: numerous cafés en route; Lloyd Hotel for lunch; Greetje for dinner

Points of interest
Muziekgebouw aan 't IJ
Venetië Hof
Lloyd Hotel
De Gooyer (windmill)
Amrâth Hotel

programme of classical music, jazz, dance and theatre, the building has a café with a large terrace on the water in the summer. A little further on is the Passenger Terminal Amsterdam, with its asymmetrical, curved glass roof. At this point, the footpath dips down to the left of the cycle path. Follow this to the tram stop, but just before you do, look over the water to **NEMO science centre**, the impressive building on your right, which resembles the hull of a ship rising up out of the water.

Walk round the tram stop and straight on to the traffic lights. Cross here and turn immediately left, taking the road that passes through Pakhuis De Zwijger (warehouse; **31**) and continues over the Jan Schaeffer Bridge (**32**) to **Java Island**. At the other side of the bridge, take the steps on your right down to water level. Turn left onto Javakade and walk the length of the island. On your left you will see neat rows of new-build apartments, interspersed with small canals where the residents can moor their boats. These canals connect to the IJ, so you will have to cross a series of pretty footbridges. On the other side of the water is a mixture of new buildings and old warehouses, most of which have now been renovated and turned into apartments, offices and cafés. There are benches at regular intervals along Javakade if you want to stop to admire the view.

Cross Bogortuin, a small grassy area at the other end of the island, and head towards the main road and tram tracks. Turn left, cross Azartplein and bear right onto Surinamekade. You are

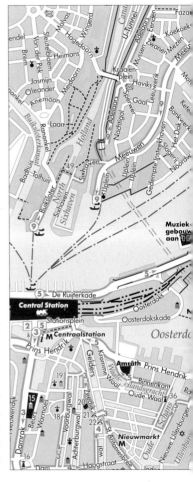

now on **KNSM Island**, looking in the other direction across the IJ to Amsterdam North. Walk straight ahead to the end of this island, where you will see the unusual, round **Venetië Hof (33)** apartment building, designed by renowned Dutch architect Jo Coenen. Go round this building and take a right on Levantkade, walking down the other side of the island. At the end of Levantkade, a short flight of steps will take you up onto the Verbindingsdam Bridge. Cross the water and follow the road round to the right. At a small junction, head right past the Brazilië shopping centre onto the Oostelijke Handelskade.

A few hundred metres/yards on, cross the road onto Rietland Park. On your right is **Lloyd Hotel** (**34**; see page 67). Continue along Rietland Park and turn right at the tram tracks towards the big junction with the prominent wooden table sculpture on the corner. Cross the junction and head under the train tracks onto Czaar Peterstraat. Still a little rundown, this street is changing rapidly, with new businesses opening their doors all the time. These include coffee and tea specialist Kaffa at number 130. At the other end of the street, you will see **De Gooyer** on your left, one of the few remaining windmills in Amsterdam. At the base of it is Brouwerij 't IJ, a small brewery that is open for beer tastings and tours between 15.00 and 20.00.

Carry straight ahead onto Sarphatistraat, and after about 100m/yds you will see a gateway on your right. Turn here and head towards the row of warehouses on **Entrepotdok**. Now apartments and offices, these warehouses were built in the first half of the 19th century as temporary storage for goods that entered Amsterdam by boat but were due to be shipped on.

Montelbaans Tower, with NEMO in the background

There are 96 warehouses in total, 84 of which are named after Dutch or Belgian cities in alphabetical order, the remaining 12 after the months of the year.

Follow Entrepotdok right onto Laagte Kadijk and almost immediately left onto **Kadijksplein**. This pretty square is lined with restaurants, the most notable of which is Café Kadijk, a tiny place that dishes out good Indonesian dinners (and lunches in the summer) on Dutch blue and white crockery.

Cross the bridge opposite Café Kadijk, turn left onto Rapenburgerplein and take the first right (Rapenburg) to the main road. You want to get to the continuation of Rapenburg directly opposite, but have to turn left and cross the main road at the traffic lights. At the end of Rapenburg take the first left onto Peperstraat. Right on the corner is **Restaurant Greetje (35**; see opposite).

Just over the bridge take the first right onto Oudeschans. Cross the canal at the following bridge, but stop in the middle to enjoy the view. On your left is De Sluyswacht, formerly the lockkeeper's house, now a cosy bar that looks like it is about to topple over. On your right is the stout **Montelbaans Tower (36)**, an old watchtower.

On the other side of the canal turn right, walk past the tower, over the next bridge, and take the first left onto Binnenkant. Follow this to the end, where you will see the imposing **Amrâth Hotel** on the corner. Built between 1912 and 1916, it is thought to be the first complete example of the Amsterdam School style of architecture. In 2007, it was converted into a 5-star hotel. It is a pleasant place for a light lunch or coffee (although the prices reflect its 5-star status), but the real reason to visit is the wonderfully preserved interior, particularly the stunning stained-glass panels showing maritime scenes in the roof of the stairwell. From the hotel, it is a short 5-10 minute walk left along Prins Hendrikkade back to **Central Station**.

Restaurant Greetje

Named after the owner's mother, Greetje is located in a beautiful old building right on the Uilenburgergracht canal. The menu is made up of French classics and updated traditional Dutch dishes, with delightful names like 'hot lightning', 'farmer's boys' and 'naked babies in the grass'. There's a strong emphasis on high-quality local and seasonal ingredients, some of which are organic, but all of which are as natural as possible. This makes Greetje not only a great restaurant but also one of the best places in Amsterdam to try Dutch food. Greetje is open for dinner on Sundays, when many restaurants are closed.

RESTAURANT GREETJE
Peperstraat 23-25
(020 779 7450
www.restaurantgreetje.nl
Open: Tue-Sun 17.30-22.00 (until 23.00 on Sat) €€€

menu with a strong Dutch flavour

starters include toasted Frisian sugar bread served with duck liver pâté and old-fashioned Dutch apple syrup

main dishes inspired by Holland's long coastline and fertile farmland — several fish and seafood dishes, pheasant or venison (in season); **vegetarian options** based on so-called 'forgotten' vegetables such as parsnips or black salsify

desserts — liquorice ice cream, stewed pears, selection of Dutch cheeses; 'Grand Finale' (for two): a sampling of all the sweets — a chance to try a little bit of everything

---

Lloyd Hotel

Lloyd Hotel has had a chequered past. Opened in 1921 by the KHL shipping company, it offered emigrants heading for the Americas a place to stay while they were waiting to embark. Used as a prison in WWII by the Germans, and later as artists' studios,

restaurants

eat

> **LLOYD HOTEL**
> Oostelijke Handelskade 34
> (020 561 3636
> www.lloydhotel.com
> Open: daily 07.00-22.00 €-€€
>
> **menu** focuses on Dutch specialities and international classics
>
> for **lunch**, a selection of egg dishes, sandwiches, soups, salads and pasta
>
> extensive **snack** menu includes cheese and charcuterie platters, croquettes and *bitterballen*
>
> **desserts** and **sweets** ranging from home-made chocolate cake and fig tart to ginger bavarois and lemon pannacotta

the building became a hotel again in 2004. All the hotel's 117 rooms are different and range from 1-star simplicity to 5-star luxury. The spacious, high-ceilinged hotel restaurant is open to non-guests and is an unusual place for a light lunch, snacks (croquettes, *tramezzini*) or coffee and home-made cakes. Also open to the public is the Cultural Embassy above the restaurant, where you can find out about cultural events taking place in the city, and the library on the fourth floor. Each floor offers a view down onto the dining area (see photograph on page 7).

The dining room at Lloyd Hotel (top) and their Dutch apple pie. For their recipe (opposite), use firm apples (Elstar, Granny Smith) which retain their shape when cooked. Packets of vanilla sugar are widely available in Dutch supermarkets. If you are unable to find it, you can make your own by slicing a vanilla pod lengthwise and burying it in a small (300-400 g) jar of sugar for at least a week before using.

Lloyd Hotel's Dutch apple pie

Apple pie is probably Holland's most famous pie. Served in thick slices, often with whipped cream, it is a popular afternoon treat or dessert.

In a large bowl, quickly combine the flour, butter, sugar, egg and salt. Knead with a mixer with a dough attachment or by hand into a smooth pastry. Leave to rest in the refrigerator for 30 minutes.

In the meantime peel, core and roughly chop the apples and mix with the sultanas, cinnamon, vanilla sugar and custard powder.

Pre-heat the oven to 180°C, 350°F, gas mark 4. Grease a 24 cm cake tin (with removable bottom) with butter. On a lightly floured surface, roll out three-quarters of the pastry into a round 4 cm bigger than the base of the tin. Transfer the pastry to the tin and press down over the bottom and up the sides.

Spread the apple mixture over the pastry and press down firmly. Roll out the remaining pastry and cut into 1.5 cm strips. Arrange in a crisscross pattern over the top of the apples, pressing the edges of the strips and the base together. Brush the pastry with the beaten egg yolk.

Bake the pie for 60-70 minutes or until the pastry is golden brown and the apples just soft. Take out of the oven and leave to cool in the tin for 30 minutes before removing and serving.

Ingredients (for about 10 slices)

450 g white flour, plus extra for rolling out the pastry
300 g butter, plus extra for greasing the tin
240 g white caster sugar
1 egg
pinch of salt

For the filling

1 kg firm apples
100 g sultanas
2 tbsp cinnamon
100 g vanilla sugar
1 tbsp custard powder
1 egg yolk, beaten

recipes

eat

Starting at the green expanse of Westerpark, this walk takes in the ornate Amsterdam School architecture of the little-visited Spaarndammerbuurt and the waterfront houses and restaurants of the Western Dock. The walk ends at Haarlemmerplein square, which hosts an organic market on Wednesdays.

westerpark & spaarndammerbuurt

WALK

Alight from the tram or bus at Haarlemmerplein and walk left round the former city gate on the western side of the square. Cross Nassauplein at the next traffic lights and follow Haarlemmerweg to the drawbridge over the canal.

The walk starts here, at the entrance to the **Westergasfabriek**. Built in 1883, the 14-hectare complex was used as a gas works until the 1960s. After full renovation, the beautiful Dutch Renaissance-style buildings reopened in 2003 as a cultural centre with

Distance: 6km/3.7mi; 1h45min

Grade: easy; on well-maintained paths throughout and walkable all year round

Equipment: see pages 12-13; sun protection

Transport: 🚊 3, 🚌 18, 21 or 22 to Haarlemmerplein; return from the same place

Refreshments: De Bakkerswinkel at the start of the walk, Café-Restaurant Open partway along the route for lunch or dinner

Points of interest
Westergasfabriek
Museum 't Schip
Spaarndammerbuurt
Bickersgracht

adjacent park. Just on the other side of the bridge is the **Regulateurshuis**, which controlled the supply of gas to the city. It is now **De Bakkerswinkel (37)** bakery and café (see page 77), a nice spot for pre-walk fortification. Walk past the buildings on your left and take the second left, Gosschalklaan. It is not marked, but it is the road closest to **Westerpark**. This large expanse of landscaped nature is popular with joggers, picnickers and young families and is at its prettiest in spring when the trees around the edge of the park burst into bloom.

Walk straight on towards the impressive silver bulk of the round **gas tank (38)**. Just past this, and before the bronze

The distinctive tower on 't Schip. The building was designed by Michel de Klerk in 1919 for the working class and contains 102 dwellings, a small meeting hall and post office. Compared to the cramped, poky accommodation the working class had previously had to endure, De Klerk's construction was regarded as a palace for the proletariat and heralded a major shift in social housing.

sculpture by Herman Makkink of a man and a woman sitting on a globe that has been sliced in half, turn right over the bridge and straight ahead past the **petting zoo**.

Go under the train tracks and past the **St Barbara cemetery**. Walk straight ahead where the road becomes a footpath. Follow this down to the main road and turn right under another railway line. On the other side of the Amsterdam Art Hotel with its brightly painted Frisian cows out front, take the first right onto Zaanstraat. You are now in the **Spaarndammerbuurt**, a neighbourhood built towards the end of the 19th century to house workers from the nearby docks. It is still mostly residential, but the main reason to visit is the Amsterdam School-style **Museum 't Schip (39)**. You will know you are going in the right direction when you see a large red-brick apartment building, with a distinctive tower, strangely bulging corners and sloping windows, on your left.

The block is fully occupied today and most of it is not open to the public. While the museum organises hourly tours of one of the restored residences (open Tue-Sun 11.00-17.00; www.

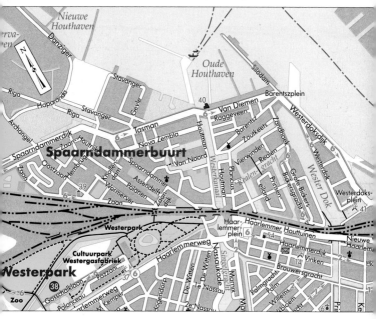

hetschip.nl; tours on the hour, every hour, €7.50), it is the building's exterior that is most impressive. So it is perfectly possible to skip the guided tour and make your own (free) circuit of the building, admiring all the unexpected and often exuberant embellishments. At the far end of the housing complex turn left. This is where you will find the museum ticket office and shop if you would like to visit, otherwise cross the road and head into the leafy Spaarndammerplantsoen square. The buildings surrounding the square were also designed by De Klerk but were built slightly earlier than 't Schip.

Westerkeer lock in operation

At the far side of the square continue onto Knollendamstraat. Turn left at the end of this and then right at the traffic lights onto Tasmanstraat. You will notice some white block-like apartments with coloured Plexiglas strips on the left. These are **student residences**. Each unit is made from a 24-metre container with built-in cooking and washing facilities. The entire complex — over 700 units — went up in 12 months and, as it is only temporary (the site will eventually be used for a new commercial and residential estate), the containers can be easily dismantled again.

Continue to the bridge over Westerkanaal, on the far side of which is an asymmetrical, green structure. This is the operating post for the **Westerkeer lock (40)**. Built in 2004, it had to comply with various regulations, one of which was that it had to offer the lock operators an unobstructed view. This explains the large window overlooking the canal and the side window that gets progressively smaller as it extends towards the back of the building.

On the other side of the bridge, the road becomes Van Diemenstraat. On the right are four buildings whose facades have been painted with **oversized maps and nautical images**. They were commissioned by the borough council and are based on historical engravings and maps from the Scheepvaartmuseum (Maritime Museum). The former grain silos on the peninsula jutting into the water at the end of Van Diemenstraat have been converted into apartments and business units. The patchwork design of **Silodam**, the last building, is a reference to the colourful container ships that regularly pass on the IJ.

As the road bends right it becomes **Wester-doksdijk**, another new housing project. But on Westerdoksplein, the square at the end of the development, is an antidote to all this newness. Perched on a section of an old railway bridge and entirely encased in glass is the understatedly elegant **Café-Restaurant Open** (**41**; see page 78). On the far side of the square turn right onto Westerdok. As you walk along the water the contrasting architecture becomes clear. All the houses on your right were built in the last few years, while the many narrow houses with ornate facades on your left are typical of 17th-century Amsterdam.

New and old along Westerdok

At Barentszplein, turn left and left again onto Bokking-

Guido Geelen's gold guitar between the arches of the railway bridge

hangen (later Zandhoek). You will cross two old wooden bridges before you come to a cobbled street on your right — beautiful **Bickersgracht**. Even without the cobbles, the snug terraced houses and communal gardens overlooking the canal make this street feels like it belongs in a village and not a capital city.

At the end of Bickersgracht, turn right and walk under the railway once again. The spaces under the arches of the bridge have been converted into shops, studios and galleries. Between the arches, artist Guido Geelen hung **35 golden sculptures** of busts, instruments or familiar objects, such as a keyboard or computer screen, as a reference to the many creative activities that are conducted here to the rumble of passing trains.

Go straight ahead at the traffic lights and take the first right onto Haarlemmerdijk. Walk to **Haarlemmerplein** at the end of the street. A small **organic market** is held on the square every Wednesday. Amsterdam's two other organic markets are both on Saturday (see page 20 in the Introduction), which makes this a good place to stock up on organic produce if you are visiting during the week. On the far side of the square catch the tram or bus to your final destination.

De Bakkerswinkel

De Bakkerswinkel bakery and café is part of a small but growing chain. But you wouldn't guess it to look at it from the outside.

DE BAKKERSWINKEL
Regulateurshuis, Polonceaukade 1
(**020 688 0632**
www.debakkerswinkel.nl
Open: Mon-Fri 09.00-18.00; Sat-Sun 10.00-18.00 €

breakfast served until midday — yoghurt with muesli, croissants, fried eggs and bacon with sourdough bread, and a small selection of sandwiches

lunch — soups, salads, quiches and hearty sandwiches (try the one filled with pastrami, sauerkraut and mustard)

sweet and savoury **high tea** served between 14.00 and 16.00

De Bakkerswinkel is housed in the old Regulateurshuis, which once controlled the supply of gas to the city.

Located in a charming Dutch Renaissance-style building at the entrance to Westerpark, this branch turns out lovingly cooked quiches, seasonal soups, sandwiches made from thick slices of home-baked bread, scones, pastries and cakes.

The place fills up quickly at weekends and is popular with young families. In fine weather, there is additional seating outside at the back of the building, otherwise ask for your food as a take-away and escape to a quiet spot in the park.

restaurants

eat

Café-Restaurant Open

'God created the Earth, but the Dutch created the Netherlands', goes the old saying. In other words, in this crowded country existing land is used efficiently, and old spaces are given new uses. When those run out, a canal is covered, a lake drained or a dike built to create more land. That was the approach taken to the old railway bridge on Westerdoksplein, which lost its function when the nearby shunting yard closed. The city council decided this piece of prime real estate shouldn't go to waste, issued a restaurant licence and organised an architecture competition.

The result is a modern, glass-encased structure (see opposite) balanced on top of the existing bridge, which has been swung into a permanently open position (thus the restaurant's name). Inside, the long, narrow space is divided in two by the kitchen and bar area. The entrance is reached via a walkway which also serves as an elevated terrace. Service can sometimes be slow, so allow yourself time for a leisurely meal at this unique spot.

The menu at Open is unfussy and elegant. It comprises elements of Dutch, French and Italian cuisine with an emphasis on sustainably caught fish, free-range meat, and the so-called 'forgotten' vegetables like celeriac. For smaller appetites, some dishes can be ordered as half portions.

CAFÉ-RESTAURANT OPEN
Westerdoksplein 20
(**020 620 1010**
www.open.nl
Open: daily midday-17.00 and 18.00-22.30
€€

starters — from a 'simple' bowl of celeriac soup to langoustines served with lemon verbena mayonnaise

mains ranging from a rich wild boar bourguignon with potatoes in winter to pan-fried plaice with wild mushrooms and creamy leek mash in summer

desserts include comforting rhubarb crumble served with crème fraîche sorbet and parfait flavoured with *appelstroop* (Dutch apple syrup, usually spread on bread)

wine list features several organic vintages and some unusually good, reasonably priced house wines by the glass

Classic crème brûlée

French food has a strong presence in the Netherlands, some say (rather unfairly) because the country doesn't have its own cuisine. Crème brûlée is an example: some chefs personalise it by flavouring with star anise or garnishing with fruit, while others give it a Dutch twist by adding *kruidkoek* (spiced cake). This recipe from Open is the classic, unadulterated French version, made with just four ingredients.

Put 250 ml of the cream with the sugar and vanilla pod in a saucepan and bring slowly to the boil. Remove from the heat and gradually whisk in the rest of the cream and the egg yolks. Leave to cool and put in the fridge overnight to allow the flavours to blend.

Discard the vanilla pod, give the cream mixture a final whisk and divide between six ramekins.

Preheat the oven to just 96°C, 205°F, gas mark 1/4 and cook for 45-50 minutes until just firm. Leave to cool, sprinkle with sugar and caramelise the surface with a blowtorch. (Or put the crème brûlées under a hot grill for about five minutes — but watch closely so that the sugar doesn't burn.)

Ingredients (for 6 people)
1 l heavy cream
9 egg yolks
1 vanilla pod
150 g sugar, plus a little more
   for the topping

recipes

eat

79

Just south of the centre is De Pijp, a bustling neighbourhood of cafés, restaurants and the famous Albert Cuyp Market. But the highlight of this walk is nearby Vondelpark, Amsterdam's green lung. A network of paths, ponds and — unexpectedly — wild parrots make this a lovely place to stroll.

de pijp & vondelpark
WALK

This walk starts at **Marie Heinekenplein**, a semi-circular 'square' in De Pijp next to where you alight from the tram. Like many of the streets in this neighbourhood, the square is named after a Dutch artist, who in this case was also the niece of Gerard Adriaan Heineken, founder of the eponymous beer company. The former brewery (now the 'Heineken Experience') is behind the red apartment building on the northern side of the square. Walk diagonally across the square, turn left

Distance: 5km/3mi; 1h30min

Grade: easy; on well-maintained paths throughout and walkable all year round

Equipment: see pages 12-13; sun protection

Transport: 🚊 16 or 24 to Stadhouderskade; return on 🚊 1, 2, 5, 7 or 10 from Leidseplein

Refreshments: numerous cafés and restaurants en route and food stalls on Albert Cuyp Market; Blauw for dinner

Points of interest
Albert Cuyp Market
Museumplein
Vondelpark
Blue Teahouse

along Quellijnstraat and right onto Eerste van de Helststraat. Where this street continues on the far side of Gerard Douplein is IJscuypje. Little more than a hole in the wall, this tiny establishment serves some of the city's best ice cream in the summer, and hearty mashed potato dishes in the winter.

At the next crossroads, turn left onto Albert Cuypstraat where the popular **Albert Cuyp Market** sets up every day of the week except Sundays. This is the place to go for everything from bicycle locks to cheap toiletries. However, there is also a large number of food stalls. Stock up on essentials such as fruit, vegetables, fresh herbs, cheese and fish at very reasonable prices. Or sample some of the ready-prepared foods that you can eat on the move. In particular, look out for herring, which is eaten raw, often with chopped, raw onions; *Vlaamse frites*, thick-cut Belgian chips that are fried to crispy perfection and served with a generous dollop of mayonnaise; and *stroopwafels*, thin waffles filled with sticky treacle.

At the end of the market, turn right onto Van Woustraat and take the second right onto Tweede Jan Steenstraat. This runs past pretty **Sarphatipark**, named after the 19th-century doctor and reformer Samuel Sarphati, whose statue can be seen in the middle of the park.

On the other side of the park the street turns into Eerste Jan Steenstraat. **De Pijp** was built in the 19th century to relieve overcrowding in the centre of Amsterdam. The neighbourhood doesn't have the quaintness of the canal belt, but it is perhaps for this reason that it feels more lived-in and less like a museum piece.

Cross over the bridge onto Balthazar Floriszstraat. At the end of it, bear left round the curvaceous red-brick apartment block on your right and head right down Van Baerlestraat. Just past the traffic lights you'll see the **Concertgebouw** (Concert Hall) on the left. Opened in 1888 on what were then the marshy outskirts of the city, the Concertgebouw is today internationally renowned for its wonderful acoustics and varied programme of classical, jazz and world music. Free concerts are given every Wednesday lunchtime at 12.30. On the right is **Museumplein**, which is surrounded by Amsterdam's major museums: the (National) **Rijksmuseum**, **Van Gogh Museum** and **Stedelijk** (Municipal) **Museum**. At the time of writing the Rijksmuseum (www.rijksmuseum.nl) had only one wing open and the Stedelijk (www.stedelijk.nl) was temporarily homeless due to refurbishment. *If you are planning a visit to either of these museums please check their websites for up-to-date information!*

A few hundred metres/yards further on, Van Baerlestraat is intersected by P C Hooftstraat. The section of the street on the right is lined with international luxury brands, but you should head left along the street, which ends in **Vondelpark**. The most central of all Amsterdam's parks, this 120-acre expanse of grass, copses and lakes, named after the Dutch poet Joost van den Vondel (1587-1679), is popular with cyclists, joggers and sun-worshippers alike. It is also the assembly point for an enthusiastic group of in-line skaters who gather here on Friday evenings to start their 20-kilometre or so skate through the city. In good weather hundreds of skaters can turn up, some bearing stereos, which gives the event a real party feel. Roads on a predetermined route are closed to traffic and it is quite a sight to see the skaters come whooshing by.

Bear left onto one of the main paths going through the park. When you see the **Blauwe Theehuis** (**42**; Blue Teahouse), a round flying saucer-like structure on your right, take the smaller path that heads over a blue footbridge towards it. Built in the 1930s in the

Blauwe Theehuis

functionalist 'Nieuw Bouw' style, this teahouse serves sandwiches for lunch, simple soups and pasta dishes for dinner (from Thursday to Saturday), and finger food for in between. With around 700 seats, including those on the first floor that provide an elevated view of the park, it also has one of the largest terraces in the country. Don't be surprised to hear squawking or see a flash of bright feathers go by as you sip your coffee. These are the offspring of a pair of parrots that escaped in the 1970s and now live in the park permanently.

After leaving the teahouse, follow the path left past the **Open-air Theatre (43)**. The theatre's future is uncertain due to funding issues, but if it survives you may see free theatre and music performances during the summer months. Head left onto the main path you were on when you entered the park and stay on it until you reach the exit gates at the southern end of the park. It is not advisable to walk through the park after dark.

You are now on Amstelveenseweg. If you cross the road and walk a few minutes to the left you will reach **Blauw (44)**, a restaurant serving top-notch Indonesian food in modern surroundings (see page 88). Otherwise, turn right along Amstelveenseweg and follow it until it becomes Overtoom.

There are also plenty of places to refuel along **Overtoom**, including Toasty! (number 437) and Dish Global Kitchen (number 255), both good lunch options, and Addis Ababa (number 337), an Ethiopian restaurant where your choice of dishes is served on a large *enjera* pancake which you eat with your hands. (This restaurant can serve gluten-free bread, pancakes and beer if ordered a day in advance.)

Almost at the end of Overtoom, turn right onto Eerste Constantijn Huygenstraat and take the second left onto **Roemer Visscherstraat**. Starting at number 20 is a row of seven houses built in the 19th-century architectural styles of seven different countries. The house at number 26, for example, is in the style of an Italian palazzo, the Russian house at number 28 is topped with an onion-shaped dome, and the final house in the row resembles an English cottage. At the end of Roemer Visscherstraat, bear left on Tesselschadestraat and then right on Vondelstraat. Follow this straight on over the Singelgracht canal, to reach **Leidseplein**.

The Moorish-style Spanish House

Restaurant Blauw

Offering a taste of the Netherlands' colonial past, Blauw is the new face of Indonesian cuisine in Amsterdam: sleek, without being pretentious, it serves authentic à la carte dishes as well as a *rijsttafel*. A Dutch adaption of an Indonesian banquet, *rijsttafel* ('rice table') consists of an array of small dishes — rice, curry, satay, vegetables, pickles and so on — served at the same time, rather like Spanish tapas. At Blauw, they are beautifully presented in white, boat-shaped bowls that just seem to keep on coming and offer the best way to sample this rich, spicy cuisine.

The restaurant also offers a fun gimmick: at the end of your meal, the waiter will ask if you want your photo taken. If you would like a souvenir of the evening, you can be snapped for free and download the result from the website the next day.

RESTAURANT BLAUW
Amstelveenseweg 158-160
(020 675 5000
www.restaurantblauw.nl
Open: Mon-Thur 18.00-22.30; Fri 18.00-23.00; Sat 17.00-23.00; Sun 17.00-22.30 €€-€€€

Indonesian **menu** that gives authentic dishes a modern twist

starters vary from *udang goreng* (crispy prawns served with a sweet, a spicy and a fragrant sauce), *loempia* (spring rolls) and *soto ayam* (aromatic chicken soup)

classic **mains** include *daging rendang* (spicy beef stew), *ayam madu* (chicken in a honey-soya sauce) and *ikan masak pedas* (fried fish with a spicy sauce)

additional **side dishes** can be ordered, such as chicken, pork or goat satay and *gado gado* (a mixed vegetable salad dressed with peanut sauce — tasting so much better than it sounds!)

highly recommended **dessert** of black rice pudding with pandan ice cream and coconut milk

---

restaurants

eat

Indonesian *nasi goreng* (fried rice)

Indonesian food has had an important place in Dutch cuisine since the days of the Dutch East India Company in the 16th and 17th centuries, and many dishes are still referred to by their Indonesian names. This recipe for fried rice is a popular example.

Cook the rice according to packet instructions, drain and set aside.

In a large frying pan, heat 1 tbsp of the oil. Pour in the egg and make a thin, well-set omelette. Remove from the frying pan, roll up and slice thinly. Put to one side.

On medium, heat the remaining oil in the pan and add the soy sauce, oyster sauce and chilli paste. Fry until fragrant, about 2 minutes. Then add the onion, garlic, pepper, shrimp and peas and, stirring continuously, fry until all the ingredients are cooked but still have a slight crunch, 3-5 minutes.

Finally, add the rice and stir until the shrimps and vegetables are evenly distributed and the rice is warmed through. Add a little more oil at this point if the frying pan is getting too dry.

Serve in four bowls, garnished with strips of omelette — perhaps accompanied by Indonesian prawn crackers (*kroepoek*).

Ingredients (for 4 people)

400 g white long-grain rice
3 tbsp sunflower oil
3 eggs, beaten
2 tbsp soy sauce
1 tbsp oyster sauce
1 tsp chilli paste
1 small onion, chopped
3 cloves garlic, minced
1 yellow or orange pepper, finely sliced
250 g shrimp (or chicken, cubed)
125 g peas, fresh or frozen

recipes

eat

This walk takes you into the little-visited eastern neighbourhoods of Oost and Watergraafsmeer. These combine a lively mix of leafy parks — both sculpture-rich Oosterpark and stately Frankendael Park — ethnic shops, pavement cafés and the bustling Dappermarkt.

oost & watergraafsmeer

WALK

This walk starts on the southern side of the **'Stopera'**, a modern colossus on **Waterlooplein** that accommodates the City Hall and Muziektheater, home to the Nederlands Opera and National Ballet. The construction, which was completed in 1986, was vigorously opposed because historic Jewish buildings had to be demolished to make way for it. During protests against the plans, the building was nicknamed 'Stopera', a contraction

Distance: 6km/3.7mi; 1h45min

Grade: easy; on well-maintained paths throughout and walkable all year round

Equipment: see pages 12-13; sun protection.

Transport: 🚋 9 or 14, or metro 51, 53 or 54 to Waterlooplein; return the same way

Refreshments: numerous cafés en route. Hartog's bakery for coffee or lunch; Restaurant Merkelbach for lunch or dinner

Points of interest
Skinny Bridge
Oosterpark
Dappermarkt
Frankendael Park

of 'stop' and 'opera', a moniker that has stuck.

With your back to the building, head down the eastern side of the **River Amstel** to the **Magere Brug** (Skinny Bridge; **29**). This much-photographed wooden drawbridge is beautifully lit at night (see page 56) and is covered in more detail in Walk 4.

At the main road head left around the **Amstel Hotel (45)**, go under the bridge, and continue walking along the river on what is now Weesperzijde. At Eerste Oosterparkstraat, turn left. Cross Wibautstraat and **Hartog's (46)** is at Ruyschstraat 56, a few doors up to the left. This family bakery is something of an Amsterdam institution. Well over a century old, Hartog's has built its reputation on wholemeal bread, made from flour that is

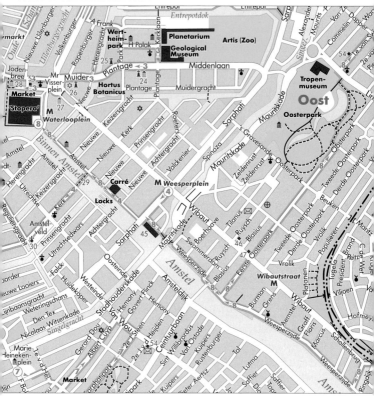

still milled on the premises. Pass by on a Saturday morning, and you will see a line of people snaking down the street, waiting patiently for one of the distinctive flat-topped loaves. Whole-meal flour also forms the basis of the bakeries' other products, which include apple pie, *ontbijtkoek* (a moist gingerbread eaten

at breakfast), and *gevulde koek* (pastry with a marzipan filling). These, plus sandwiches, fresh juices and coffee, are also available at the shop and café **Hartog's Boterham (47)** at Wibautstraat 77 (open Mon-Fri 07.00-16.00; Sat 08.00-16.00). *No Hartog's products are gluten-free,* but you could make your own sugar bread using the recipe on page 104.

After a few hundred metres/ yards, Eerste Oosterparkstraat meets and runs down one side of **Ooster-park** (East Park). Enter the park through the gate about half way down its length. Turn right along the footpath and then take the path on the left that skirts the small lake. In front of the perimeter fence just before the lake are several statues. One shows three figures on a bench. They are Koekebakker, Hoyer and Bavink, the Little Titans who appear in the book of the same name by Dutch author Nescio. The other is 'The Scream', created by artist Jeroen Henneman to represent freedom of speech and to commemorate the outspoken writer and film-maker Theo van Gogh, who was murdered near the park in November 2004.

The Scream

You will exit the park on Linnaeus-straat, from where you should just be able to see the copper-topped spires of the **Tropenmuseum** (Tropical Museum), a treasure trove of colonial artefacts from the East Indies and Africa. Just to the left of the exit is Eerste van Swinden-straat. Walk along here and take the first right onto Dapperstraat. Every day of the week except Sunday this street hosts the **Dappermarkt**, a lively food and clothing market.

At the end of Dapperstraat (the last part does not have a market on it), turn left past the fire station onto Domselaerstraat, under Muider-poort Station, and bear right around Oosterspoorplein square. On the far side of the square turn right and take the first left, Tergouwstraat. Continue on to J C Breenstraat. This entire area is currently being developed, and large plots of cleared ground have been fenced off with brightly coloured boards. A footpath has been left open, however, so it should be quite clear when you reach the end of J C Breenstraat that you need to turn left and shortly thereafter right, through the middle of the building site and on towards the canal.

Cross the footbridge over the canal and turn right along Linnaeuskade. Take the third road to the left, Linnaeusparkweg, and the first right off the pretty roundabout with a fountain in the centre. At Middenweg cross the road and you will see **Frankendael Park** on your left. The park was created in the early 17th century when the Watergraafsmeer lake, which gives this neighbourhood its name, was drained. The park was extensively restored at the turn of this century and is now a mix of wide-open, grassy spaces and landscaped gardens.

A few minutes walk left along Middenweg is **Restaurant Merkelbach** (**48**; see overleaf). It is located in the former coach house of **Huize Frankendael**, a country estate dating from 1660. To reach it, go through the gleaming entrance gate, decorated with the head of Mercury, the Roman god of trade, on the front, and the coat of arms of the Gilde-meester family, the house's owners in the 18th century, on the back.

Huize Frankendael, home to Restaurant Merkelbach

To return to the city centre, walk back along Middenweg and at the Ringvaart canal turn left onto Ring-dijk. The canal is higher than the houses so, for the best views, walk up the steps to the footpath running along the top of the dike. At the end of the dike cross Wibautstraat, go under the train tracks and bear left onto Schollenbrugstraat. You regain Weesperzijde, but further down. Turn right and walk all the way back along the River Amstel to the **'Stopera'**, where you can catch trams and metros onwards.

Restaurant Merkelbach

Located in the coach house of a former country estate in Frankendael Park, Restaurant Merkelbach serves up atmosphere and a French-Mediterranean menu for breakfast, lunch and dinner. Seasonal, organic ingredients are used where possible, and vegetarians are well catered for. Behind the restaurant is a terrific terrace overlooking the house's extensive garden, carefully restored in Regency style based on old prints and drawings.

The recipe opposite (illustrated below) is an example of Merkelbach's seasonal culinary approach; it uses both green and white asparagus, which are traditionally eaten from early May to June 24, the feast of Saint John.

RESTAURANT MERKELBACH
Middenweg 72
(**020 665 0880**
www.restaurantmerkelbach.nl
Open: daily 08.30-23.00 €€

French-Mediterranean **menu**; classic dishes with a modern twist

baguettes, paninis or sourdough sandwiches for **lunch**; also salads, soups, and heartier fare like pasta

dinner entrées such as duck confit seasoned with Moroccan Ras el Hanout spice mix or lemon sole with onion compote, raisins, pine nuts and rucola; **mains**: lamb with potatoes, turnips, pancetta and garlic gravy or vegetarian lasagne drizzled with pungent herb sauce

desserts — blood orange with lemon mousse, mint and marmalade; chestnut and almond cake with mascarpone cream and dates; selection of cheeses

restaurants

eat

Asparagus salad with broad beans and poached egg

Bring two large saucepans of salted water to the boil. Peel and cook the white asparagus *al dente* (this only takes a few minutes). Remove from the heat and leave to cool in the cooking water.

Peel the green asparagus and shell the beans. Put both into the other saucepan and blanch. Cool immediately in ice water. Drain all the vegetables. Slice the asparagus into three pieces and mix with the beans in a large bowl. Wash and drain the salad.

For the vinaigrette, mix the vinegar, mustard and sugar in a bowl. Slowly add the oil and whisk until the dressing is thick and smooth. Season with salt and pepper to taste.

Dress the salad, asparagus and beans. Divide the salad between four plates and heap the asparagus and beans next to it. Put a small piece of goat's cheese on each crouton and arrange on the salad.

On a low heat, bring another saucepan filled with about 2 inches of salted water to the boil. Add a dash of vinegar and break the eggs into the water. Cook for 1 minute, remove the saucepan from the heat and leave the eggs to stand for a further 5-6 minutes until just firm. Remove each egg from the water with a slotted spoon and place on top of the asparagus.

Garnish with chopped chervil and serve.

Ingredients (for 4 people)

8 white asparagus
8 green asparagus
1 kg broad beans (in their pods)
2 slices soft goat's cheese
12 ready-made croutons
100 g mesclun mixed salad
4 fresh eggs
1 small bunch chervil

For the mustard vinaigrette

2 tbsp white wine vinegar
1 rounded tsp coarse mustard
pinch of sugar
5 tbsp sunflower oil
salt and freshly ground black pepper

recipes

eat

No trip to Amsterdam would be complete these days without a visit to Amsterdam North, the upcoming neighbourhood located a short ferry ride away across the IJ, and a fascinating combination of new cafés, neat rows of houses, industrial estates and old dikes.

amsterdam north

WALK

Start the walk at **Central Station**: walk through the main station building to the back exit on De Ruijterkade. Cross the road, and the blue and white GVB ferries to Amsterdam North should be clearly visible on your left. Take any of the ferries going to Buiksloterweg. These are free and run at least every 12 minutes, 24 hours a day. When you get off the ferry, walk straight ahead until Buik-

Distance: 7km/4.3mi; 2h

Grade: easy; on well-maintained paths throughout and walkable all year round

Equipment: see pages 12-13; sun protection

Transport: any 🚌, 🚐 or metro to Central Station; return the same way

Refreshments: limited cafés en route; dinner in Hotel de Goudfazant

Points of interest
North Holland Canal
Nieuwendammerdijk
Vliegenbos

sloterweg bears left. You want to take the footpath in front of you that leads to the **Willemsluis locks (49)**. Cross over the **North Holland Canal** via the narrow walkways on top of the locks. The canal was built in the 1820s at the request of King Willem I, after whom the locks are named, to accommodate larger ships coming in to Amsterdam's harbour via Den Helder. It was replaced only half a century later by the much deeper, and shorter, North Sea Canal.

Follow the footpath on the other side of the locks. Just before it joins the main road, you will see two odd-looking tapering towers on your left — these provide ventilation for the motorway tunnel under the IJ that connects central Amsterdam with Amsterdam North. Take the path that goes left round the towers. Cross the motorway and walk up to the pavement that

Amsterdam North's industrial face

runs in front of the houses on Adelaarsweg — don't follow the red cycle path directly adjacent to the motorway.

Cross Kraaienplein and walk along the continuation of Adelaarsweg on the other side of it. As you walk north, you will notice that the motorway is getting further away, the street is becoming quieter and the surroundings more rural.

At the roundabout take the second exit to the right, **Nieuwendammerdijk**. This lovely, narrow street (shown on page 98) has a real village feel to it. The traditional buildings on it, which are a combination of wooden dwellings from the 16th century and *kapiteinshuizen* from the 17th century (so called because they were bought as retirement homes by well-to-do captains), provide a sharp contrast to the modern architecture that dominates this part of Amsterdam.

Just before the church, turn right onto Nieuwendammerkade. There is a small yacht harbour here and several grand, two-storey houseboats, the likes of which are rare in the crowded centre of Amsterdam. By the lone grey office building, the road makes a sharp turn to the right and becomes Zamenhofstraat. After a couple of hundred metres/yards it turns into

Vliegenbos

Volkstuinen Buitenzorg

Noord

Java

IJ Hav

Muziek-
gebouw
aan

Dijksgracht

Dijksgracht

De Ruijterkade

Central Station

NEMO

a footpath that skirts the **Vliegenbos** wood on the right and the **Volkstuinen Buitenzorg** allotments on the left.

At the far side of the wood the path leads you round the Technical School and Bredero College buildings and up to Meeuwenlaan. Walk left along the main road, cross over the roundabout with the ESSO service station on the corner and take the first left onto Schaafstraat. By the Opel dealer you will see a dead-end sign next to the road, but immediately underneath it another sign saying 'except Hotel de Goudfazant'; in this unlikely culinary neighbourhood, this is a useful indication that you are in the right place.

Shabby-chic: Hotel de Goudfazant, with its spectacular chandelier

Follow the street round to the left, where it becomes Aambeeldstraat, and then take the first right down towards the waterfront. **Hotel de Goudfazant** (50; see opposite) is the last building on the left.

To return to central Amsterdam, retrace your steps to the beginning of Schaafstraat. Turn left onto Meeuwenlaan and walk all the way to the end of it, where you can catch the IJplein ferry, also free (runs at least every 15 minutes from 06.00-midnight), back to **Central Station**.

Hotel de Goudfazant

Situated in the unlikely surroundings of an industrial estate, Hotel de Goudfazant used to be a garage. Little has been done to the spacious interior since then, bar the addition of a spectacular chandelier made out of transparent bottles. In these shabbily chic surroundings, the chefs turn out excellent, affordable food, and the tables set up on the waterfront in warm weather offer great views of the city across the IJ.

HOTEL DE GOUDFAZANT
Aambeeldstraat 10H
(020 636 5170
www.hoteldegoudfazant.nl
Open Tue-Sun 18.00-01.00 €€

regularly changing **menu** that combines Dutch and international influences

good choice of **starters**, including a salad of duck confit, Puy lentils and lardons; cream of celeriac soup with smoked sprat and chervil

mains comprising several seafood dishes, including risotto with marinated octopus and seaweed; whole roasted poussin served with potatoes and chunky apple and rhubarb compote; inventive **vegetarian** options, such as strudel filled with pumpkin, aubergine, spinach and almonds

desserts — Dutch favourites, such as *hemelse modder* (literally 'heavenly mud' — chocolate mousse), as well as bread and butter pudding, pecan pie with plum and Armagnac ice cream, and a selection of cheeses served with fig relish

Roast poussin at Goudfazant

restaurants
eat

Hartog's sugar bread

Sugar bread is made from a rich dough prepared with sugar cubes. As the bread cooks, the cubes form sticky pockets in the loaf. This recipe from Hartog's bakery (Walk 8; see page 91) also includes nuts and candied peel, which complement the sweetness. It is a delicious breakfast option, spread with butter, or use it as the basis for a luxurious version of *wentelteefjes* (French toast, see page 33).

Heat the oven to 140°C, 275°F, gas mark 1. Spread the nuts on an oven tray and roast for 45 minutes. Remove and leave to cool.

Grate the rind of the lemon and squeeze out the juice. Mix the rind and juice with half the sugar.

On a clean work surface, mix together the flours, remaining sugar, butter, cinnamon, salt, candied peel and lemon mixture.

Form the ingredients into a mound, make a well in the centre, and pour in the water. Dissolve the yeast in the water with your fingers and, little by little, incorporate the flour-butter mixture. Knead the dough for 10-15 minutes until all the ingredients are well mixed. Add up to an additional 60 ml of water if necessary — the dough should feel firm but no longer sticky.

Ingredients (for 1 loaf)

- 80 g nuts (mix of cashews, almonds and hazelnuts)
- 2 lemons
- 40 g cane sugar
- 500 g wholemeal flour
- 50 g white flour
- 50 g butter
- 5 g ground cinnamon
- 10 g salt
- 50 g candied peel, finely chopped
- 300 ml cold water
- 30 g fresh yeast or 14 g dried yeast
- 320 g cane sugar cubes

recipes

eat

recipe • **sugar bread**

Knead in the nuts and sugar cubes. Form the dough into a ball, cover with a warm, damp tea towel and leave to rise in a draught-free spot for 30-45 minutes, or until it has increased in size by 1/3.

Remove the tea towel, punch the air out of the dough and knead again briefly. Form into a loaf and place in an oiled bread tin about 10 x 25 cm (4 x 10 in). Cover with a warm, damp tea towel again and leave to rise for at least another 30 minutes or until it has again increased in size by 1/3.

Preheat the oven to 220°C, 425°F, gas mark 7. Put the bread in the oven and reduce the temperature to 200°C, 400°F, gas mark 6. Bake for 35-40 minutes — or until the loaf is golden brown and sounds hollow when you tap on the bottom of it. Remove from the tin and allow to cool completely on a cooling rack.

Starting just south of the aptly named Rivierenbuurt (River District), this walk takes you through Amstelpark and out of the city, along the banks of the Amstel, to the picturesque village of Ouderkerk aan de Amstel. The river winds past grand old houses, windmills and fields, with plenty of places to refuel at the end of the walk.

along the river amstel

WALK

10

The walk begins at **Station RAI**, where you take the Europaboulevard exit. Turn right and follow the silver and blue signposts pointing the way to **Amstelpark**. At the intersection with A J Ernsstraat turn left, cross the road, and the entrance to the park is just in front of you (open daily from 08.00 until half an hour before sunset).

Amstelpark, one of the few bike-free spots in Amsterdam, was created in 1972 for the Floriade, a major horticulture festival that is held in a different location in the

Distance: 6.5km/4mi; 2h

Grade: easy; on well-maintained paths throughout and walkable all year round

Equipment: see pages 12-13; sun protection

Transport: 🚌 4 or metro 50 or 51 to RAI. Return from Ouderkerk aan de Amstel on 🚌 146 or 175 via Bijlmer Arena Station (see page 112)

Refreshments: limited cafés en route but several options in Ouderkerk aan de Amstel itself, including De Oude Smidse for lunch or dinner

Points of interest
Amstelpark
De Riekermolen (windmill)
Statue of Rembrandt
Wester-Amstel country estate

Netherlands once every ten years. After the Floriade had finished, it was decided to keep the exhibits — which included a Belgian Monastery Garden, a Japanese Garden and an Israeli Biblical Garden complete with desert — as intact as possible. As a result, the park is home to a great diversity of native and foreign flowers, plants and trees.

From the entrance gate, take the main path that bears to the right. You can stay on this path for the length of the park, until you reach the southern exit (signposted 'De Borcht' or 'Uitgang'). However, you can easily branch off left or right and take

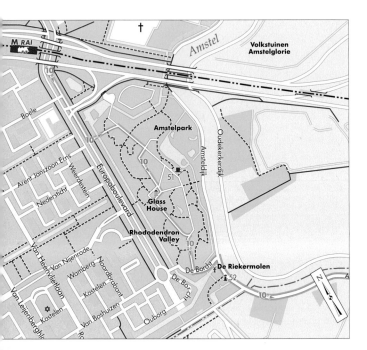

in some of the sights the park has to offer before returning to the main path. Het Glazen Huis (The Glass House), for example, regularly holds exhibitions. The building is not always open, but as all the walls are composed almost entirely of glass you can admire the artworks from outside. The Rhododendron Valley is also worth a detour, particularly in April and May when the 8000 bushes burst into riotous bloom. In the middle of the park is **De Hop (51)**, a café with a basic selection of sandwiches, cakes, ice creams and drinks, toilets, and a pleasant lakeside terrace (open daily from 10.00 until the park closes).

At the park's southern exit, turn left onto De Borcht and walk towards **De Riekermolen**. This windmill, shown on page 106, dates from 1636 and was used up until 1932 to drain the Rieker polder (reclaimed land) in the nearby village of Sloten. When a centrifugal pump was introduced after 1932, the windmill lost its function but has been well maintained, despite being dismantled and reassembled in its current location in 1961. You can't visit the interior, but it is still a popular photo-op stop for passing coach and bicycle tours.

Next to the windmill is a **statue of Rembrandt (52)**. It shows the artist kneeling on one knee and making a sketch of the river and countryside, something he often did in this area. Continue past the statue onto Amsteldijk, the road running alongside the **River Amstel**. The river is a relatively quiet place for rowing crews to train, while the rural surroundings are popular with walkers, runners

Het Glazen Huis: the walls are almost entirely made of glass.

and cyclists. The proximity to Amsterdam also makes this a very desirable area to live, and the majority of the houses (most of which are private residences) are large and detached. **Wester-Amstel** at number 55, however, is open to the public.

House beside the Amstel and sculptures of geese at the Wester-Amstel property

There were once more than 50 country estates on the banks of the Amstel, where the well-to-do could escape the heat and stench of the city in the summer. Wester-Amstel, built around 1665 by a merchant, is one of only three remaining between Amsterdam and Ouderkerk aan de Amstel. The former coach house occasionally hosts concerts and exhibitions, and the small but beautifully tended park is well worth a wander (park open between Apr 15 and Oct 15 Mon-Fri during office

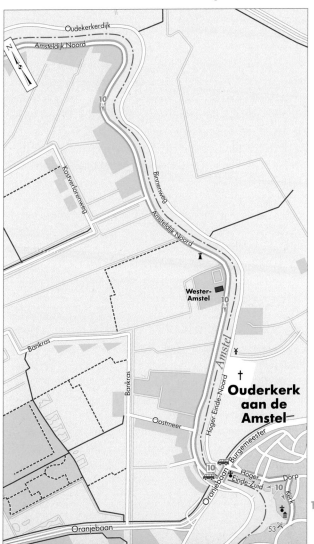

Oudekerkerdijk

Amsteldijk Noord

N

10

Kostverlorenweg

Binnenweg

Amsteldijk Noord

Wester-Amstel

10

Bankras

Bankras

Amstel

Hoger Einde-Noord

Oostmeer

† **Ouderkerk aan de Amstel**

Burgemeester

10

Oranjebaan

Hoger Einde-Zuid

10

Dorp

Kerk

Oranjebaan

53

111

hours; also open Sat-Sun 12.00-18.00; tel: 020 496 5656; free entrance).

Just before **Ouderkerk aan de Amstel** a bridge spans the river. There are several cafés and restaurants in the village that serve drinks, snacks and full meals. None of them falls into the budget category, and service seems to be slow across the board. However, many have large terraces right on the river which means that at least there is plenty to look at while you wait! The easiest places to reach, and thus also the busiest, are those clustered just past the bridge. These include Brasserie Paardenburg, Praq and Loetje aan de Amstel.

For something a bit quieter and in the heart of the village, turn left at the bridge onto Oranjebaan. Cross the river and take the first right onto Hoger Einde-Zuid. This becomes Dorpstraat. Take the first right, Kerkstraat, walk past the church and over the old-fashioned drawbridge. **De Oude Smidse** (**53**; see page 114) is on the right.

To get back to Amsterdam, retrace your steps to Oranjebaan. There are bus stops, both called Brug/Amsteldijk, just before and after the bridge. Take bus 146 or 175 to **Bijlmer Arena Station**. The buses run four times an hour during peak times and twice an hour at other times from 06.00 to 19.30 (146) or 22.30 (175). From Bijlmer Arena Station (not shown on the map), take the metro back to your final destination.

Or — instead of getting the bus, for a real leg-stretcher you can also walk back to Amsterdam along the even more rural eastern bank of the river. It is worth noting, however, that the first place to cross the river again is at the A10 ring road (there

Ouderkerk aan de Amstel: if service in the many cafés and restaurants is slow, there is at least plenty to watch on the river!

is a separate path for cyclists and pedestrians). This runs along the northern edge of Amstelpark and will take you back to **RAI Station**, where you started.*

*If you have a good city map (this stretch is not shown in the book), you could also turn off right under the ring road *before* RAI Station and walk past the **Volkstuinen Amstelglorie** allotments. Cross the footbridge over Duivendrechtsevaart, a side canal that joins the Amstel, and walk past the **old water tower** to Spaklerweg Station. Turn left, cross the small roundabout and carry straight on to **Amstel Station**. From here catch tram 12, metro 51, 53 or 54 or mainline trains to your final destination.

De Oude Smidse

A former smithy, cartwright's workshop and inn were joined together to form this atmospheric restaurant in the centre of Ouderkerk aan de Amstel. In the winter you can dine inside by an open fire and in the summer outside on the sunny waterside terrace. Like the majority of restaurants in the village, De Oude Smidse tends towards the expensive end of the price range. Prices are matched by the quality, however, so it should be a satisfying splurge.

DE OUDE SMIDSE
Achterdijk 4
(**020 496 1262**
www.deoudesmidse.nl
Open: Tue-Sat 12.00-00.00
(kitchen open until 21.30) €€-€€€

Dutch/French **menu**, with the occasional foray further afield

for a light **lunch** — bruschetta, sandwiches made with toasted Turkish bread; salads. Three-course lunch menu also available

starters — smoked salmon terrine; king crab with melon and Dutch shrimp; lasagne made with goat's cheese

mains range from local leg of lamb with risotto and tomato gazpacho to whole-roasted French chicken served with home-made piccalilli or monkfish fried in Japanese tempura, served with basmati rice

for **dessert**, opt for a plate of local cheeses or choose from a selection of ice creams and sorbets

restaurants

eat

Endive mash

Stamppot or mash is a popular winter warmer — easy and very versatile. Instead of endive, you could use curly kale (*boerenstamppot* or 'farmers' mash'), sauerkraut (*zuurkool stamppot*) or cooked carrots and onions (*hutspot*). Bags of ready-prepared endive (*andijvie*) are available in Dutch supermarkets, as are floury (*kruimig*) potatoes and an impressive selection of smoked sausages (*rookworst*).

Put the potatoes in a pan, cover with cold, salted water and bring to the boil. Reduce the heat and cook until soft, about 15 minutes.

Warm the sausage as per the instructions on the packaging.

Drain the potatoes in a colander but leave the cooker on. While the potatoes are draining, warm the milk and butter in the empty saucepan, add the potatoes and mash until smooth.

Add the endive and stir into the mash with a wooden spoon until it is warm and wilted, about 5 minutes. Add salt and pepper to taste and the nutmeg.

Slice the sausage and place on top of the mash. Serve with apple sauce and/or mayonnaise.

Ingredients (for 4 people)

1.5 kg floury potatoes, cut into chunks

400 g endive, washed and finely chopped

1 x 350 g smoked cooked sausage

1 tbsp sunflower oil

150 ml milk

50 g butter

salt and freshly ground black pepper

pinch of nutmeg

recipes

eat

This walk, the longest in the book, is well worth the extra exertion — to experience the shady copses, fragrant pine forests and rolling dune landscape that make up a large part of the Netherlands' North Sea coast. Most of the route is through the North Holland Dune Reserve.

castricum to egmond aan zee

WALK

This walk is one of nearly 50 created by Dutch National Railways and walking organisation Stichting Wandelplatform-LAW that start and end at a railway station. A map can be picked up in Amsterdam Central Station or Castricum, but queues can be long. It's far easier to print off the **excellent free map** at www.eropuit.nl in advance. On the homepage, type Castricum into the 'Zoek een uitje' search box. '**Noord-Hollands Duinreservaat**' will be one of the options returned. Click on the photo and scroll to the bottom of the page for a link to the map (*kaart*) in PDF format. Usefully, the map also shows picnic benches along the route if you want to bring your own food. The accompanying route description is currently only available in Dutch, but the notes below will assure you don't get lost!

Start the walk as you

Distance: 15km/9.3mi; 3h30min

Grade: moderate; can be muddy on the paths and windy on the coast

Equipment: see pages 12-13; sun protection, waterproof walking shoes, windproof jacket, swimming costume and towel to swim/sunbathe

Transport: 🚐 from Central Station to Castricum (every 15 minutes; for exact departure times and more information on planning your journey, see page 14). Buy a day return ticket (around €10). Return from Egmond aan Zee on 🚌 164 to Castricum train station (daily at about 50min past the hour; between 14.00 and 19.00 (Sat/Sun 18.00) also about 25min past the hour)

Nature reserve ticket: most of this walk is through the North Holland Dune Reserve, for which you need a ticket (adults €1.50; children up to 15 free). The machine at the entrance accepts all coins from 10 cents upwards but does not give change.

Refreshments: at the beginning, end and 5km/3mi into the walk; Restaurant Van Speijk or MiraMare for snacks or lunch

Points of interest
North Holland Dune Reserve
North Sea coast
Egmond aan Zee

alight from the train in **Castricum**, a small town about 40km/25mi northwest of Amsterdam. Go down off the platform and turn right under the tracks (*don't* follow the signs for Centrum). At regular points along this walk you will pass square red and white markers which indicate the way to different destinations with details of their distance. In general, however, you will be following the route marked by red and white '**NS wandeling**'® stickers/arrows.

At the station car park, turn right and, just past the old farm building, turn left onto Kramersweg. At marker P-21400 walk straight ahead onto Onderlangs, and then turn right onto the cycle path. At marker P-62399/002 turn right along the concrete wall. At Geversweg turn left. A little further up this road is a **ticket machine** where you can buy tickets for the **Noord-Hollands Duinreservaat** (North Holland Dune Reserve), one of the largest areas of natural beauty in the country.

At marker P-22590 bear left onto Hogeweg. This runs through a small copse whose floor is covered with wild flowers in the spring. Continue straight ahead onto Nieuweweg. At the next fork turn left and walk straight ahead onto Oude

Schulpweg. In the 17th and 18th centuries this was one of the paths used by **mollusc fishermen** to transport their carts loaded with shells from the coast to Castricum. Here, the shells were loaded onto boats and taken to nearby Akersloot where they were burned in kilns to produce lime. This was used as a component in mortar. Stay on Oude Schulpweg for almost a kilometre, cross the paved road, and continue along the same path to its end.

Turn right along the sealed Bredeweg. At the bend by marker P-22594, head right again onto the unsealed path. After 20m/yds you will meet the **Hollands Kustpad** (Dutch Coastal Path). Follow this to

Pretty copse with a bench; below: winter walking on the dunes

the right. You are now out of the forest and in **De Limiet**, a grassy dune area used for grazing cattle and sheep. At Johanna's Weg, the sealed road at the far side of this area, turn left. After 200m/yds turn left again onto Groeneweg.

At the Groeneweg/Johanna's Hof crossing (marked on a stone next to the path), turn right and cross the sealed path. Cross Leplaan and, at the end of the path, head left past

Johanna's Hof

Johanna's Hof. This was once a farm, one of several that were built here in the early 19th century when an attempt was made to turn the dunes into land suitable for agriculture. It was soon discovered that the ground was not very fertile and the water supply unreliable; the attempts were abandoned. Johanna's Hof is now a large café/restaurant, popular with young families who come to visit the animals in the adjoining paddocks, and the only place for refreshments until the end of the route. The large terrace makes it a nice place to stop for a drink, but there is a much better choice of food in Egmond aan Zee.

On the other side of Johanna's Hof cross the main road and turn right along the footpath. About 200m/yds further on, turn left onto Van Speijklaan, the cycle path that heads into the forest. Turn right onto Dennenlaan and, just through a gate, turn left onto Kroftlaan. At the stream (this does not always have water in it), turn left onto the path that runs alongside it. At the next opportunity, turn right and cross the stream. Where you emerge from the forest at the end of this path, turn left and, at the sealed Staringweg, turn right. Go straight ahead at marker P-22887 and take the first right directly after an open area of dunes. Turn left at the next crossing and almost immediately right, back into the forest. Turn right at the paved road and take the first left back through the forest.

When you emerge onto another dune area, turn right. Follow the path through a **fragrant pine wood** and turn left onto a track partly sealed with bricks. Cross Van Oldenborghweg and follow Lageweg upwards. You will stay on this path for almost 2km/1.2mi as it winds through dunes covered here and there with scrubby grass, low bushes and flowers such as wild pansies, which are better able to withstand the persistent sea winds than trees.

Cross Middenweg and continue along Lageweg. Where the pine trees end, take the rising path on your left. A little further along this path, two wooden handrails mark the entrance to a **bird-watching hut** that overlooks a small lake. The reserve is rich in bird life and, depending on the time of year, you may see stone chats, kingfishers, nightingales, bitterns and several birds of prey (eagles, vultures, goshawks), to name a few. At the

Wild pansies and the bird-watching lake

crossing with a stone marker ('Egmond-Binnen 3km'), turn right along Vlewoscheweg. Where the path descends you should get your first glimpse of **Egmond aan Zee** through the dunes on your left. After the bench, turn right and head towards the houses. As you approach the town you will see several square pits dug out of the surrounding dunes. These are typical of the coastal villages here and were used by the inhabitants as vegetable plots, meadows or bleaching fields for their fishing nets. Some are still used today for livestock, while others serve as a place for kids to kick around a ball.

At the main road, Churchilllaan, turn left, walk to the other side of the car park and take the shell-covered path towards the sea. Take the walkway down to **the beach** and walk right. This wide stretch of sand is popular all year round — in the summer with sunbathers and at other times with kiteflyers, watersports fans and walkers. It can get crowded, particularly at weekends, but the place has an unhurried feel, unlike Amsterdam. If you fancy spending a few hours here or want to cool off with a dip in the sea, you can change and lock up your belongings in one of the beach huts. These can be rented from Bad Egmond, one of the beach pavilions about ten minutes walk along the beach. A sandy path next to Bad Egmond takes you up to the boulevard on the seafront. You can walk quite some way along the boulevard, exploring the lighthouse and more of the town, but you will need to return to this point to get to the bus stop.

Restaurant Van Speijk (see opposite) is on the left as you come off the beach. Or try MiraMare on the other side of the road, an Italian restaurant that serves thin-crust pizzas and pasta dishes and does a roaring trade in home-made ice creams.

To return to Amsterdam, walk straight along Voorstraat, the street running down the side of MiraMare, for about 500m/yds. The **bus stop** is opposite the **tourist information office** (VVV).

Restaurant Van Speijk

Restaurant Van Speijk is set back from but overlooking the sea and serves food that is a cut above the fare to be found in the pavilions just on the beach. The interior is a slick mix of black and

RESTAURANT VAN SPEIJK
Westeinde 1
(072 507 1703
www.restaurantvanspeijk.nl
Open: daily 11.00-21.30 €-€€

international **menu** with some Dutch favourites — *broodje kroket* (croquette in a bun), chicken satay and chips, and *poffertjes* (baby pancakes with icing sugar) — thrown in for good measure

for **lunch** there is a choice of sandwiches, omelettes and salads, including the 'Egmondia': lettuce with Dutch shrimp, crayfish and smoked salmon

the **snack menu** is longer than most and includes local Beemster cheese, smoked sausage with mustard, tuna sashimi and chicken teriyaki.

silver — somewhat at odds with Egmond aan Zee's relaxed resort feel — but the large, protected terrace is an ideal spot to catch the sun and rest your feet while enjoying your meal.

restaurants

eat

This excursion to Muiden, a short bus ride east of Amsterdam, begins with a visit to the medieval castle of Muiderslot. The interior and grounds make for a great day out, but there's more for walkers — a scenic 10km circuit from Muiden to Muiderberg through open pastures and back to Muiden along an old sea dike.

muiden & muiderberg

EXCURSION

On arrival at Muiden Park & Ride, cross the main road and follow the green signs for Muiderslot castle. This will take you through the village of Muiden and eventually to the **Grote Zeesluizen** (Large Sea Locks). Cross the locks and turn left on Herengracht, which ends at the entrance to the castle.

Muiden lies at the mouth of the **River Vecht**, where it empties into the IJmeer lake. The lake used to be the Zuiderzee (South Sea) and was the only way for ships to reach Amsterdam and other destinations on this side of the North Holland peninsula before the much deeper and shorter North Sea Canal was built in the late 1800s. The sea became a lake in 1932 when the 30-kilometre IJsselmeer Dam and road link that connects North Holland and Friesland opened.

Transport: 🚋 12 or metro 51, 53 or 54 to Amsterdam Amstel Station. Follow the signs for the buses and take the exit marked 'Julianaplein'. Take 🚌 152 or 157 (towards Almere); departures half-hourly, but staggered, so that you should never have to wait more than 15 minutes. Alight at Muiden Park & Ride; journey time 16min. For more information on timetables and planning your journey see page 14 in the Introduction. Return to Amsterdam the same way.

Refreshments: ample cafés/restaurants; Graaf Floris V van Muiden recommended (see page 133).

Points of interest

Muiden

Muiderslot castle (see opening times on page 127)

De Kazerne (barracks)

Recommended walk: Muiderberg Route, 10km/6.2mi; 2h30min; easy; but can be windy and muddy on the unsealed dike path after it has rained. See 'What to take' on pages 12-13: you will need sun protection, waterproof walking shoes and a windproof jacket. Refreshments are available at the start/end of the route (at Muiden), as well as halfway along (at Muiderberg), but not in between.

Muiden is over a thousand years old, and although it is small and sleepy today, its once-strategic location means it has a rich history. **Muiderslot** itself was built around 1280 by Floris V, count of the provinces Holland and Zeeland. After the count was murdered in 1296 the castle was largely destroyed, but was rebuilt around 1370 and adapted numerous times thereafter.

Amsterdam

Amstelijk

Ams

A10

A2

River Amstel

Walk 10

Muiderslot: the castle was opened to the public at the end of the 19th century. The grounds are lovely, with shady walk-ways (as shown be-low), a plum orchard and a well laid-out herb garden.

The castle's most famous inhabitant was the writer and poet Pieter Corneliszoon Hooft, who lived here during

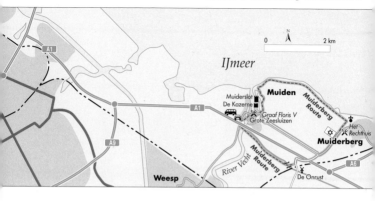

the 17th century's Golden Age. Visitors are free to explore most of the castle themselves, but a separate guided tour takes in the furnished part of the fortress where Hooft resided. For a time the castle was also part of the **Stelling van Amsterdam**, a 135-kilometre defence line circling the capital, made up of a network of forts and batteries and an ingenious system of locks that could be opened to flood large areas of land.

Castle open Nov-Mar weekends only 12.00-17.00; the rest of the year Mon-Fri 10.00-18.00; Sat-Sun 12.00-18.00. Admission €11 adults/ €6.25 children 4-11 years, including guided tour. Payment by cash and Dutch PIN cards only).

If you're doing the walk, head back from Muiderslot to the locks to get to the start. Look for the hexagonal green and white sign for the **Muiderberg Route** on

the corner of Graaf Floris V van Muiden's terrace. You will be following these signs for the duration of the walk. The route is generally well marked, but there are a few occasions where the signs disappear or are not immediately obvious, so I have included directions (see overleaf) and a sketch map on page 127.

Before you leave Muiden, don't miss **De Kazerne**: from the locks walk east along the main road (Naarderstraat), then turn left into Kazernestraat. De Kazerne were the barracks that formed part of Muiden's defences; they are now a library. The back of the

Muiden: entrance to De Kazerne and (left) an old ship near the Large Sea Locks

barracks is hidden under a mound of earth and grass, but you can admire the 19th-century facade, shown above. There are (very clean) public toilets in the building that cost €0.20 (the doors are coin operated and only accept 20 cent coins).

To return to Amsterdam, follow the green signs for 'Parkeerplaats P1'. These will take you back over the locks, left along

Muiderberg Route

From the hexagonal sign on the corner of Graaf Floris V van Muiden's terrace, follow Herengracht straight on past the restaurant and out through the southern side of the village towards the A1 motorway. Walk under the A1, cross the road and take the grassy path that runs along the top of the dike.

Just under 2km along, at the railway lines, turn left over the wooden bridge and walk parallel to the train lines on the sealed footpath. You should just be able to see windmill **De Onrust** ('the commotion') on the other side of the tracks. Built in 1809, it is said to have got its name from the creaking and thumping noises it made as it pumped water out of Naardermeer lake. It is still in use today. Where the path ends and meets the road, turn left and cross over the A1 — there is no footpath until after the traffic lights on the other side of the bridge.

At the traffic lights, walk straight ahead into **Muiderberg**. Note that the footpath here also doubles as a cycle path, so look out for bicycles. Just outside the village is a **Jewish cemetery**. It has been a burial ground for the High German (Ashkenazi) Jewish community since 1642 and is the largest Jewish cemetery in the Netherlands. As you enter the village, you will see **Het Rechthuis** on your right. In the early 20th century, when the lake was still the Zuiderzee, Muiderberg was a popular seaside

The Muiderberg Route, a 10km circular, signposted route created by the ANWB (Royal Dutch Tourist Association) takes you through open farmland between the two villages — with plenty to see en route.

resort, particularly with Amsterdammers who arrived in droves on the **Gooische Steam Tram**. The tram, which was nicknamed the Gooische Murderer because of the number of road deaths it caused, terminated at this point, and Het Rechthuis served as the station and waiting room. It is now a stylishly renovated hotel and restaurant where you could stop for a drink or lunch.

Het Rechthuis

Opposite Het Rechthuis is a small park (this is the official starting point of the Muiderberg Route, as you can see on the map next to the path). Walk through the park and follow the route signs to the exit in the far left corner. Pass the small church and at the car park take the footpath up onto dike. The wind blowing off the **IJmeer** (one of the reasons the lake is popular for watersports) can make it very bracing up here — but you have a fine view out over the water to the right and open pastures with grazing livestock and buildings to the left.

Past the white house built right into the dike you should see Muiderslot appearing again on the left. A couple of hundred metres/yards before the castle there's a final fence. There is no route sign, but you should see a red and white arrow-shaped sticker pointing towards the left. Get down off the dike and follow the path round the small lake. Where this path joins the road, the route signs appear again and direct you right over a bridge. Take the first right onto Ton Kootsingel and then the first left towards **De Kazerne** (see page 129). By the main entrance to the barracks take the cobbled pathway right, then the road left, between the picturesque old houses. At Naarderstraat, turn right and **Graaf Floris V van Muiden** (see page 133) is on the corner.

Muiden: the River Vecht from the Grote Zeesluizen (Large Sea Locks). The café/restaurant Graaf Floris V van Muiden overlooks the scene.

Weesperstraat and over two green footbridges. Cross the main road and walk past the stop where you alighted, to the far end of the car park. The stop for buses 152 and 157 is just next to the bus-only slip road off the motorway. *Flag down* the bus you want — or it may not stop!

Graaf Floris V van Muiden

A restaurant and bar has stood on this spot since the Middle Ages, and history seems to ooze from every corner. The wood-panelled interior is dark and cosy, and the pictures of ships that crowd the walls pay tribute to Muiden's nautical past. The menu doesn't break new ground (perhaps with the exception of 'asparagus month'), but portions are generous, prices reasonable and service friendly. The riverside terrace provides a good view of the locks and the many pleasure boats that pass through them (see photograph opposite).

GRAAF FLORIS V VAN MUIDEN
Herengracht 72
(029 426 1296
www.graaf-floris-v.nl
Open: daily 11.00–22.00 €-€€

predominantly Dutch **menu**

special asparagus menu from the last week of April to the end of May: 5 courses (each of which can be ordered individually) featuring the 'white gold' — even a dessert of asparagus ice cream with caramelised asparagus!

lunch — soups, pancakes, burgers and sandwiches (the triple-decker club sandwich is particularly good)

snack menu includes deep-fried favourites like *kaastengels* (pastry straws filled with melted cheese), *bitterballen* (round, ragout-filled croquettes), apple pie

fish and meat dishes (fried cod, spareribs, pork medallions) feature large on the **dinner menu**, but there are meat-free options such as fresh pasta with spinach and sage butter, stuffed sweet peppers, goat's cheese Tarte Tatin

---

Club sandwich at Graaf Floris V

restaurants

eat

The Kröller-Müller Museum is famed for its collection of works by Vincent van Gogh, but its location in the centre of the sprawling Hoge Veluwe National Park, about 70km southeast of Amsterdam, means it offers as much to nature lovers as it does culture enthusiasts.

kröller-müller museum

EXCURSION

The museum is named after Helene Kröller-Müller, an avid art collector. It was her dream to have a 'museum home' for her 11,500 pieces, and her dream came true when the Kröller-Müller Museum opened in 1938. She died a year later.

The museum is famous for its collection, which comprises 272 paintings, drawing and prints by Van Gogh, as well as works by Seurat, Picasso, Mondrian, Gauguin and others. The permanent display is complemented by temporary exhibitions focusing on developments in contemporary art.

Transport: 🚂 from Amsterdam Central Station to Apeldoorn or Ede-Wageningen; then 🚌 108s to Rotonde Otterlo and finally 🚌 106 to Kröller-Müller Museum. Buses run once an hour. Total journey time about 1h45min. For further information on timetables and planning your journey, see pages 14-15 in the Introduction. Return the same way.

Website: www.kmm.nl

Opening times: Tue-Sat 10.00-17.00 (sculpture garden open until 16.30)

Admission: adults €15; children up to 12 €7.50; children under 6 free. Prices include entrance to the national park.

On the website (English version), under 'activities' you'll find a 'routemaker', which you can use to plan your own route through the museum. Either select eight pieces from the collection and print these out with their background information; or select a route with a specific theme, for example portraits, nudes or artworks with passion.

Next to the museum is a sculpture garden, featuring around a hundred works from the late 19th and 20th centuries by the likes of Rodin, Moore, Hepworth and Dubuffet. The sculptures have been carefully arranged across the 25-hectare area in

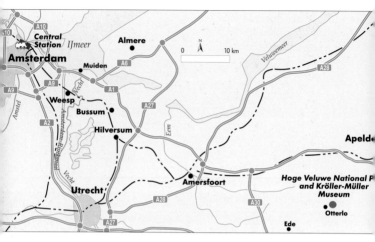

between trees, on grassy slopes or tucked away among the rhododendrons — depending on their character.

The museum alone takes several hours to explore, but if you have time there is also the surrounding **Hoge Veluwe National Park** (www.hogeveluwe.nl; English version), an additional 5500 hectares of forest, moorland, lakes and drift sand. This is home to endangered plants and animals, including the nightjar, moor frog and several butterflies. You may also encounter deer, wild boar and moufflon.

The park has mapped out a number of walks, several of which are circular. **Route maps** for these can be bought from the Visitors' Centre for a couple of euros. Another option, which enables you to see much more of the park than if you were on foot, is cycling. You can pick up one of the 1700 free **'white**

Even in winter the Hoge Veluwe is a fine place for a bracing walk, and you have a good chance of seeing deer.

bikes' at the park entrance, Visitors' Centre or museum and drop it off at any of the bicycle racks when you are finished.

The park has **two restaurants**, Monsieur Jacques (www. monsieurjacques.nl, with a menu in English) in the museum and De Koperen Kop (www.dekoperenkop.nl, no English version) in the Visitors' Centre. The former is good for a snack or light lunch, the latter offers more substantial fare suitable for any time of day — from lunch through to tea and dinner. Both are self-service and fairly spartan in décor.

Food intolerances are becoming ever more common, and we know there are a lot of you with intolerances out there. Even if you have learned to cope at home, it can be daunting to go on holiday. Will the food in restaurants be safe? Will I be able to buy gluten- and dairy-free foods? Here are some tips that should make your eating choices much simpler.

EATING IN RESTAURANTS

Dutch **breakfasts and lunches** are predominantly based on bread, and cafés and sandwich bars will invariably only offer bread made from wheat flour. If you are having breakfast out, *take your own bread*, and top with ham and eggs (cold or cooked).

Soups and salads are usually a safe lunch option, although it is always worth checking whether a soup is thickened with flour or a salad contains cheese or croutons. Look out for pea soup and brown bean soup in winter, delicious traditional Dutch soups that are usually made with gf, df ingredients.

At **dinner**, **main courses** shouldn't pose too many worries, but explain clearly what your requirements are (see inside back cover for Dutch phrases). **Desserts**, as usual, present the most problems, since they often include milk, cream, butter or cheese.

The Dutch website www.glutenvrij.nl has an English page with clickable subheadings listing places to eat or buy gf products. Several of the restaurants recommended in this

EAT GF, DF

book have been mentioned here and on various blogs about gf eating in Amsterdam, among them In De Waag, Open, Blauw.

GF, DF SHOPPING

The **Albert Heijn** supermarket chain (see page 18) has a health food section in their largest branches, of which there are not many in the centre. However, at press date **gluten-free products** were stocked at Jodenbreestraat 21 (Walk 3) and Van Baerlestraat 33a (Walk 7); look or ask for the 'Gezondheid' (Health) aisle. Here you will find an excellent assortment of those wonderful Schär goodies, as well as others from the Dutch firm Conzenza. Both shops also stock Van Rijsingen soya ice cream.

It is relatively easy to pick up **dairy-free** soya milk, yoghurt and puddings in many supermarkets; these can usually be found next to their dairy-based equivalents.

In addition, the city has a good number of health food shops and a growing number of **Natuurwinkels**, a chain of health food supermarkets, branches of which are located on or close to the routes of Walks 2, 3, 6, 7 and 8 (all numbered '54' on the walking maps). All branches of Natuurwinkel have an extensive gluten-free section that includes muesli, biscuits, cakes, pasta, crackers and partially cooked bread. The latter has to be finished off in the oven, so will only be an option for those staying in self-catering accommodation.

One other popular health food shop is **Biomarkt** (www.biomarkt.nl) at Weteringschans 133-137, very close to Walks 4 and 8 (No 55 on the plan inside the front cover). It also stocks Schär products, among others.

MENU ITEMS

aardappel potato
aardbei strawberry
abrikoos apricot
aioli garlic
   mayonnaise
ananas pineapple
appel apple
artisjok artichoke
asperge asparagus
aubergine
   aubergine
azijn vinegar
bami Chinese
   noodles
banaan banana
basilicum basil
biefstuk steak
bier(tje) beer
bitterbal ragout-
   filled croquette
bloem flour
bloemkool cauli-
   flower
boekweit buckwheat
bonen beans
boter butter
broccoli broccoli
brood bread
broodje bread roll
bruine bonensoep
   brown bean soup
bruisend/plat water
   sparkling/ still
   water

cacao cocoa
champignon mush-
   room
chocolade chocolate
chocopasta choco-
   late spread
citroen lemon
coquille scallop
courgette courgette
deeg dough/ pastry
drank drink
drop licorice
druif grape
duif pigeon
eend duck
ei egg
eiwit protein
erwtensoep pea
   soup
fazant pheasant
framboos raspberry
fris soft drink
fruit fruit
fruitsalade fruit
   salad
gamba giant prawn
garnaal shrimp
geitenkaas/melk
   goat's cheese/
   milk
gehaktbal meatball
gember ginger
gevogelte poultry
glas/fles glass/
   bottle

glucose glucose
glühwein mulled
   wine
glutenvrij gluten-free
griesmeel semolina
groente vegetable
hagelslag chocolate
   sprinkles
halfvol (melk) semi-
   skimmed (milk)
ham ham
haring herring
haver oat
heilbot halibut
hert venison
honing honey
hüttenkäse cottage
   cheese
ijs ice cream
jam jam
jenever Dutch gin
jus gravy
kaas cheese
kabeljauw cod
kaneel cinnamon
kapertje caper
kapucijner marrow
   fat pea
karnemelk butter-
   milk
kastanje chestnut
kikkererwt chickpea
kip chicken
klein/groot small/
   large

knoflook garlic
koekje biscuit
koffie coffee
koffie verkeerd caffè
   latte
kokosmelk coconut
   milk
komkommer cu-
   cumber
kool cabbage
koriander coriander
krab crab
kreeft lobster
rozijn raisin
kruiden herbs
kruidenthee herb
   tea
kruidnagel clove
kroepoek prawn
   cracker
kwartel quail
lactose lactose
lam lamb
lever liver
linzen lentils
mager (melk)
   skimmed (milk)
maïs corn
maïsmeel cornflour
makreel mackerel
margarine mar-
   garine
melk milk

GLOSSARY

mossel mussel
mosterd mustard
muesli muesli
munt mint

nasi Indonesian-style rice
noot/noten nut/nuts
nootmuskaat nutmeg
oester oyster
olie oil
olijf (olie) olive (oil)
paling eel
pannenkoek pancake
pap porridge
paprika pepper (green, yellow, red)
parelhoen guinea fowl
pasta pasta
peer pear
peper pepper
pijnboompit pine nut
pinda peanut
pindakaas peanut butter
pompoen pumpkin
prei leek
pruim plum
rijst rice
rode biet beetroot
rogge rye
room cream
rundergehakt minced meat (beef)

sap juice
saus sauce
schapenkaas/melk sheep's cheese/ milk
schelpdier shellfish
sereh lemongrass
sinaasappel orange
siroop cordial
sla lettuce
sojasaus soya sauce
spek bacon
sperzieboon green bean
spinazie spinach
spruitje Brussels sprout
stuk slice/piece
suiker sugar
taart cake/pie
tarwe wheat
thee tea
toast toast
tomaat tomato
tonijn tuna
tosti toasted sandwich
ui onion
uitsmijter fried eggs and ham on sliced bread
varkensvlees pork
vaasje small beer
vegetariër vegetarian (person)
vegetarisch vegetarian (food)
venkel fennel
vet fat

vis fish
vissoep fish soup
vla custard
vlees meat
volkoren whole-grain
vruchtensap fruit juice
wafel waffle
warme chocolade-melk hot chocolate
water water
wijn wine (*rood/wit/rose*) (red/white/rose) (*droog/zoet*) (dry/sweet)
wild game
worst sausage
wortel carrot
yoghurt yoghurt
zalm salmon
zeebaars sea bass
zetmeel starch
zout salt
zuivelproduct dairy product
zuurkool sauerkraut

SHOPPING TERMS

apple *appel*
asparagus *asperge*
bacon *spek*
beef *rundvlees* cuts:
  entrecôte *entrecôte*
  fillet *filet*

mince *gehakt*
sirloin *sirloin*
steak *biefstuk*
tenderloin *ossen-haas*
beer *bier*
bread *brood*
butter *boter*
cabbage *kool*
cake *taart*
carrots *wortels*
cauliflower *bloem-kool*
celery *selderie*
cheese *kaas*
chicken *kip*
chicory *witlof*
chocolate *chocolade*
chocolate sprinkles *hagelslag*
cod *kabeljauw*
coffee *koffie*
cornflour *maïsmeel*
courgette *courgette*
cream *room*
cucumber *komkom-mer*
dairy-free product *zuivelvrij product*
duck *eend*
eggs *eieren*
endive *andijvie*
fish *vis*
flour (wheat) *bloem*
gluten-free *gluten-vrije bloem*
fruit *fruit*
game *wild*
garlic *knoflook*

grapes *druiven*
ham *ham*
herbs *kruiden*
ice cream *ijs*
juice *sap*
kilo *kilo*
  half kilo *halve kilo*
lamb *lam*
cuts:
  chop *karbonade*
  cutlet *kotelet*
  leg *bout*
  loin *lende*
  rack *carré*
  shank *schenkel*
  shoulder *schouder*
leek *prei*
lemon *citroen*
lettuce *sla*
litre *liter*
  half litre *halve liter*
liver *lever*
lobster *kreeft*

milk *melk*
mushroom *padde-stoel/champignon*
mussels *mosselen*
mustard *mosterd*
nuts *noten*
  almonds *amandelen*
  hazelnuts *hazelnoten*
  peanuts *pinda's*
olive oil *olijfolie*
onions *uien*
orange *sinaasappel*
oysters *oesters*
parsley *peterselie*
pasta *pasta*
pear *peer*
peas *erwten*
pepper (spice) *peper*
pepper (sweet) *paprika*
pine nuts *pijnboompitten*

pork varkens-vlees
cuts:
  chop *karbonade/lap*
  cutlet *kotelet*
  fillet *filet*
  tenderloin *haas*
potatoes *aardappelen*
poultry *gevogelte*
prawns *garnalen*
  giant *gamba's*
pumpkin *pompoen*
raspberries *frambozen*
rice *rijst*
rosemary *rozemarijn*
salmon *zalm*
salt *zout*
sausage *worst*
shellfish *schelpdier*
soup *soep*

soya *soja*
spices *specerijen*
spinach *spinazie*
strawberries *aardbeien*
sugar *suiker*
tea *thee*
tomatoes *tomaten*
tuna *tonijn*
turkey *kalkoen*
veal kalfsvlees
cuts:
  cutlet *kotelet*
  escalope *oester*
  sweetbread *zwezerik*
tongue *tong*
vegetables *groenten*
vinegar *azijn*
water *water*
  sparkling *bruisend*
  still *plat*
wine *wijn*

CONVERSION TABLES

Weights		Volume		Oven temperatures		
						gas
10 g	1/2 oz	15 ml	1 tbsp	°C	°F	mark
25 g	1 oz	55 ml	2 fl oz			
50 g	2 oz	75 ml	3 flz oz	140°C	275°F	1
110 g	4 oz	150 ml	1/4 pt	150°C	300°F	2
200 g	7 oz	275 ml	1/2 pt	170°C	325°F	3
350 g	12 oz	570 ml	1 pt	180°C	350°F	4
450 g	1 lb	1 l	1-3/4 pt	190°C	375°F	5
700 g	1-1/2 lb	1.5 l	2-1/2 pt	200°C	400°F	6
900 g	2 lb			220°C	425°F	7
1.35 g	3 lb			230°C	430°F	8
				240°C	475°F	9

bold type: photograph; *italic type:* map (*ifc:* inside front cover)

INDEX 143

First edition © 2011
Published by Sunflower Books
PO Box 36061, London SW7 3WS
www.sunflowerbooks.co.uk

ISBN 978-1-85691-394-2

Cover photograph: converted warehouses on Prinsengracht (Walk 1)

Photographs: Cecily Layzell
Maps: Sunflower Books, adapted from various sources
Cookery editor: Marina Bayliss
Series designed by Jocelyn Lucas
A CIP catalogue record for this book is available from the British Library.
Printed and bound in China by WKT Company Ltd

Before you go …
log on to
www.sunflowerbooks.co.uk
and click on '**updates**', to see if we have been notified of any changes to
the routes or restaurants.
When you return …
do let us know if any routes have changed because of road-building, storm
damage or the like. Have any of our restaurants closed — or any new ones
opened on the route of the walk? (Not restaurants in the centre, please; these
books are not intended to be complete restaurant guides!)
Send your comments to mail@sunflowerbooks.co.uk